OPTIC SUBWOOF

THE
BAGLEY
WRIGHT
LECTURE
SERIES

DOUGLAS KEARNEY

OPTIC
SUBWOOF

WAVE BOOKS

SEATTLE AND NEW YORK

Published by Wave Books

www.wavepoetry.com

Copyright © 2022 by Douglas Kearney

Wave Books titles are distributed to the trade by

Consortium Book Sales and Distribution

Phone: 800-283-3572 / SAN 631-760X

Library of Congress Cataloging-in-Publication Data

Names: Kearney, Douglas, author.

Title: Optic subwoof / Douglas Kearney.

Description: First Edition. | Seattle, Washington : Wave Books, [2022]

Series: Bagley Wright Lecture series | Includes bibliographical references.

Identifiers: LCCN 2022020014 | ISBN 9781950268672 (paperback)

Subjects: LCGFT: Poetry.

Classification: LCC PS3611.E177 O68 2022 | DDC 811/.6—dc23

LC record available at https://lccn.loc.gov/2022020014

Designed by Crisis

Photo on p. 28 by @nycstreetart. Illustrations
and collage poems by Douglas Kearney.

Printed in the United States of America

9 8 7 6 5 4 3 2 1

First Edition

OPTIC SUBWOOF

"What we say we recognize when
we see ourselves seeing ourselves ..."

YOU BETTER HUSH

BLACKTRACKING A VISUAL POETICS

*For Chaun Webster, Airea D. Matthews, Tarik Dobbs,
emi anne kuriyama, Evie Shockley, Michael Demps,
giovanni singleton, Gail Swanlund, and Brooke&Brick*

"Hush."

It rushes in from out the tape hiss thicket, a sibilant imitation of silence, the fecund dark where a sonic world is sung into being. The choir breaks the hush for to hush it. What loud silence is commanded here?

A piano drags in its $A\flat$ chord an instant behind *hush*'s exhalation, making like sound has a shadow. Then, the aural field fills with the downbeat of beatdown footfalls, a four-on-the-floor stomp conjures ground down in this sudden world. These pulses spread wide the rhythm's generosity, its plentitude; the good mess of grace notes pulling and pushing what's lockstepped along, a long way from home to get to where we are.

"Hush."

Now with an $E\flat^7$ tolls the piano, the Wattsline Choir under James Cleveland keeping on. That sung chord's demand bends over the onomatopoeic order, calls shape to a vocal study in progress. The marched cadence against the stage whispered "hush" bids for quiet maneuvers in the cut. The congregants' movement must needs stay a rushed *hush-hush*. And doesn't the composition and vocal timbre tell us the chorus *is* a congregation? Harmonies familiar to the Gospel listener, a texture of Black legibility, the tugged glissando of the curved blue note.

And because "Hush, Hush, Somebody's Calling My Name"—a traditional song Quincy Jones arranged for an album inspired by *Roots*, the TV miniseries adapted from Alex Haley's book—those who recognize are meant to recognize that to hush one's steps, one's voice, one's prayer is to keep Death at bay. That to travel dark is to travel in darkness

3

when one petitions for godspeed, going on the hush to the *hush harbor*, those holy hollows where Black people could worship in secret. "Hush." Where, once there, one might hear:

> Somebody's calling my name.

And when we come to know that this "Somebody" "sounds like Jesus," this song, in the context of a group both haunted and hunted, conducts a study of hush and utterance's conundrum among the dark surveilled:

That one requires the silence of hush's harbor to keep one's flesh from death, but you'll break that silence to hear the call to a spiritual life.

> What shall I do, Oh Lord,
> What shall I do?

This lecture is about the noise that calls itself *quiet*.

This lecture is about meaning to harbor sounds of Black life in an insistent hush.

And because this lecture insists on sound Black life, it's about what it means to be cut from one context then recontextualized in another.

So:

This lecture calls itself tracing a line through collage as congregants may sing in study of quiet.

Hush, hush, again and again.

This lecture flashes what I mean to conceal when I plan to hush in plain sight, to be in the cut in the cuts that compose the poems that *cleave* and *cleave to* my previous visual poetry.

This lecture? It's about loud-assed, colored silence.

I once led a course where we searched for chimes between literature and hip-hop studio production techniques. An idea my students and I worked at in the first weeks was voice as a *signal* of *Blackness*'s presence rather than the presence of *Blackfolx* themselves.

We played tracks featuring methods and textures of Black vocal performances—rap flows saturated with regional drip, chopped soul hooks, melismatic R & B runs, Trap's disembodied ad-libs. I described how these locate *Blackness* as matter, material like burnt cork, ready to be put onto any song, any genre. Key to this idea is that "Black" *voice/voicing* becomes a metonym for Black people; we are *associated* with certain techniques such that they may come to stand in for us. Say: *urban* or *soulful*. This is proxy shit, part and parcel byproduct of slavery's forced import and exploitation's steady unbalanced export in a marketplace defined by misappropriation. The extracted voice-cum-Blackness gets packaged and shipped on some Henrietta Lacks: detached from its hush-hush source.

Leaning into the contemporary, we traced a run that included Roger Troutman's talk-box vox, Electro's vocoders, and Auto-Tune, a pitch corrector developed by Antares. These devices of articulation haven't the same long history of Black coding as blued notes or the rasp what turns "singing" to "sangin." So, in changing the texture of Black vocality, these technologies unsettle ideas of audible Blackness from their not so distant pasts. Auto-Tune's forcible corrections high-step over the bent, blued note, turning it from a slide to a chromed-out stairway. This is a serious sonic break in aesthetics. To parse it, I might-could adapt writer/theorist Kodwo Eshun's suggestion that crate-digging, sample-coveting, hip-hop beatsmiths aren't necessarily devoted musicologists but impatient with all that isn't groove. Perhaps the cut notes in an Auto-Tuned glissando might suggest a means to teleport past a traditionally sidling singing voice. From scholar and theorist Alexander Weheliye, I could call it "[reconstruction of] the black voice in relation to *information technologies*." And Auto-Tune in contemporary Black music is Afrofuturist under filmmaker/multimedia artist Cauleen Smith's rubric: it reckons with technology, reinvention, and motion.

The uncanny valley of pitch-corrected vocals associates easily with cybernetics. Posthumanity? A twenty-first-century cyborg, sure. But also: Black people as "automata" is a foundational (mis)reading of our activities. A shallow-ass deepfakkke in which the Black singing voice been an emotional prosthesis for whiteness. Its performance of sonic plentitude some aural comfort food. A signal of being taken higher, taken there, somewhere transcendent, or below woe into a drylongso Hell.

In my work, I've meant to mess with this marvel; being a Black poet bid to sing. To *hush*, without voicing "Hush." To forestall a death varietal by way of a silence. Which is to say, I've tried to compose poems *I* cannot read aloud. To re-rig a visual poetics into legit, loud-assed colored silences.

What is a loud-assed colored silence?

I figure it as a teeming field of language. A radio station that thinks it's a photograph, a collage that wants to be a palimpsest, a pen nib in the eye—poking it or jutting from it. At least that's what the loud-assed colored silences were meant to be.

I wrote seven of them for my collection *Buck Studies*. "Booming System aka Miranda Rizights," "Scat," "Beat Music," "Human Beatbox," "Modernism," "Moan," and "Protest." Each, save "That Loud-Assed Colored Silence: Modernism," nods toward a mode of utterance associated with Black culture. This is not to say that Black culture has no reflections in Modernism, only that one might not *begin* from the grounds that Modernism is, from jump, about sound.

"Loud-Assed Colored Silence" poems work a number of compositional techniques I've been at since I started my "performative typography" poems. In her essay "Trauma and the Avant-Garde," poet and critic Sueyeun Juliette Lee describes the series in general and "That Loud-Assed Colored Silence: Protest" in particular:

Presented as collaged torn and layered text with various white-outs, font sizes, and overwrites, these works are visually "loud" in a way that conjures layers of posters lining public walkways in metropolitan downtowns.... They confront the reader, asking them to abandon a conventional understanding of how a poem "should" appear on the page. These works invoke graphic design and literature.

In "That Loud-Assed Colored Silence: Protest," Kearney directly references and protests the surplus of signification that is blackness. If we imagine this work in visual layers, the base or farthest background layer references the famous civil rights protest song, "We shall overcome some-day." However, the lyrics have been transformed—some of the parts that are legible read, "We are overcome. We are all afraid." The next layer appears in the largest font of the piece; "AIN'T I AN AM?" "I AIN'T WHAT!" and "I CAN'T AIN'T!" are further emphasized by their placement in rectangular boxes.

The next layer up is composed of permutations of the now nationally recognized campaign and hashtag #BLACKLIVESMATTER, but transposed as #BLACKLIVESSTUTTER, #BLACKLIVESSTAMMER, #BLACK-LIVESYAMMER, and #BLACKLIVESMUTTER.

I composed these poems (except, again, "Modernism") using page-layout software. In nearly all cases ("Beat Music" being the only poem using the "torn" images Lee describes), I worked exclusively by typing into then arranging text boxes I planted in the poem's open field. The typeface I selected for the "body" text of the "Loud-Assed Colored Silence" series was the same as the more conventionally formatted poems in *Buck Studies*. At the time, I thought this consistency would guide readers to keep *reading* rather than switch to *looking*.

This anxiousness around whether my poems would be read versus looked at has been a part of my poetics for some time. But it wasn't until 2019 that I gained a more precise vocabulary with which to de-heebie my jeebies.

In the fall of that year, poet and scholar Evie Shockley convened Color Inside the Lines at Rutgers. In this symposium, participants assembled to discuss "Visuality and Visibility of Race in Poetry." As defined by Shockley:

Visuality [is] formal aesthetic choices that draw poetry on matters of race and ethnicity into a prioritized relation with visual culture or the visual field. *Visibility* [is] cultural legibility and social representation (how race and ethnicity might be *discernibly present* in the work, for actual or potential audiences).

Visibility, it seems to me, corresponds to *reading*. *Visuality*, to *looking*.

As a Black person in a space, I recognize my visibility, the uttered hush of it. That I am (mis)read as a present absence/absent presence: I am simultaneously here, a particular flesh and blood human; yet the materiality of Blackness absents me as a specific presence. That I am visible when an eye needs me to be where I'm wanted for my unwantedness and invisible whenever I'm not needed. I imagined the *visuality* of the "Loud-Assed Colored Silence" poems would drive readers to more actively read what's visible, drawing them in by recalibrating legibility, performing a kind of typographic shimmy. I think they've done that.

However, I also hoped they would displace my body from spaces where its legibility gets recalibrated by others. And they might have done!

But my simple ass decided to read them aloud.

And, in voicing them, I rendered them "scores," undoing their resolution as visualities. They were not "complete" until I performed them, which amplified my visibility. Every collaged voice becomes additional fleshing—my throat rasps, my diaphragm announces itself by way of sustained sounds, my head ticks to render mechanical repetitions, spit flies from my mouth. Yet, these techniques, meant to perform collage as a vocal mode, tears at the edges of my (lyric) particularity.

Here I was, meaning to be in the cut, only to start cutting up.

The history of the African diaspora is one in which brutal *de*contextu-alization followed by violent *re*contextualization are the start of our *what had happened was*. What is it to reckon with what it is to be displaced then re-placed only ever as out of place unless we've been put in *our* place?

This forced movement is similar to collage, a mode of production I have long found fascinating. Perhaps *because* it seems to chime with an idea of Black subjectivity. Perhaps it was once mere coincidence. Though for nearly thirty years, collage has been, for me, a methodol-ogy, a praxis.

Last year, however, I came out the shower, thinking on this section of this lecture. I was standing in steam, daydreaming some insight about collage. Instead, I came up with the merely provocative—

Humanity's first encounter with collage was death.

And even this was not what I legit thought. *Death* isn't necessarily *worked* since *death* can happen without a consciousness arranging it, a presence that seemed a requirement of art, which was where I was hous-ing collage. Thus:

Humanity's first encounter with collage was a murder scene.

And there we were there, I thought at the moment. A veldt's nigh monochrome invaded with the ever-red saturations of the body's inte-rior. An ancestor, making this encounter with the murder victim, draws back before leaning in. The ancestor thinks—*this body shouldn't be there.*

All that red shouldn't be out here, it's come from somewhere else and yet here it is. The decontextualization (red from the inside) forced into a new context (the outside), the standing context (a walk on the veldt's nigh monochrome) transformed as well. Nothing the same.

But my lightning bolt of euphoria fizzled to low-grade dejection super quick. Because I had bound art to murder. And for that moment it was the truest thing I could think.

But I drew back. Box Browned out. I popped and locked an escape like Richie Green from *The Last Dragon*, quitting murder to reconcile with sweet, innocent death.

> Humanity's first encounter with collage was a dead thing in an incongruent habitat.

An ancestor encounters something dead—not murdered per se—but dead, nonetheless. But here's the thing: the thing is dead where it wouldn't usually live. Hectares and hectares of the veldt's nigh monochrome and what the—a stiff catfish. Or, unfurled songbird.

The ancestor, perhaps not drawing back at all, leans in, thinking— *this shouldn't be here and yet here it is, gone from there* (i.e., water or sky).

> Humanity's first encounter with collage was a dead bird on the ground.

Again, not murdered per se. Though I've murdered it, plucked it from the sky and set it down on the ground. In my head, it is not bloody, but it is red as a cardinal, but it isn't a cardinal. It is a red-assed bird from some African place. A black-headed gonolek? A firefinch? A red bishop? Sure, fine, okay. But it's dead. I won't say hunted. I didn't find it, but made it *dead*, here, for this—an *illustration*.

And why not the fish? Which is to say:

Humanity's first encounter with collage was a dead fish on the ground.

Well, how does the fish get all the way here in the veldt's nigh mono-chrome? That is narrative. Not collage.

Humanity's first encounter with collage was a dead bird on the ground.

It's easier to imagine a sky thing dropping to the ground than a water thing getting there somehow.

I brushed my teeth thinking about the difference between a murder scene and a place where death is what had happened was. Whether de-contextualization to recontextualization in a context required a hand to do the cutting, to make mobile the cut bird, the bird cut—wings flared —from the sky, to their splayed tragedy on the nigh monochrome of the veldt floor. This was some business and would be about when my an-thropocentric chauvinism was set to flower in full—the bird plucking being mere lubrication for the privileging of art and will, in cahoots with a necropolitical power to kill. And top that off with a pearly jam of what I figure is masculinist toxin—that art comes when someone else is made to bleed for it. Murder traded to a bird falling because bird's die some-times, not by stones. But there was Death calling, calling, wearing maybe an ecru skull, not an off-white one.

What shall I do?

Humanity's first encounter with collage was a flower blooming where none had before.

Hush, Death! And flowers somehow rhyme with dead birds, their petals like down or feathers, no? Something, something spring, right? When my mouth was full of toothpaste, I wasn't thinking masculinist, that's me now, fifteen minutes later, trying to sound intelligent or just virtuous. I was thinking about anthropocentricity, though. Dead-ass.

But what's the deal with me sprouting flowers to evacuate a masculinist space? I give myself some side-eye. And at this point now I'm composing in real time. All the way live. I'm sitting at our dining table. There's a dog underneath it, but she's our dog, so. There is an unpaid medical bill. A flashlight. This laptop. My mother-in-law is setting up her coffee and a bottled water. She lives with us, so. There's a postcard of my baby cousin. My glucose test kit. This is not a collage. This is just a mess. And will remain that as long as we insist on eating and dropping bills here.

The ancestor wants me to regain focus. They right, they right.

Humanity's first encounter with collage was a flower blooming where none like it had before.

How free of flowers had the nigh-monochromatic veldt been *prior* to this lone blooming in order for it to *feel* like a new contextualization of field? Must the ancestor's familiarity with the flower be such that they recognize it as coming *from* somewhere else and not just new *here*?

That collage could occur without human intervention. Let's pick that red bird back up off the nigh-monochromatic veldt floor. Blackheaded gonolek, let's get you back—what? You prefer hunting around in the undergrowth? Then it wouldn't be surprising to find you there on the ground in the first place? Why didn't you—? Fine. You: firefinch? Your name is awesome. The firefinch is back in the sky. And—what is it, red bishop? *Veldts describe terrain in southern Africa and that's where you're from,* while the firefinch—? Well, what if it's a *red-billed* fire-finch?

Let's pick that red-billed firefinch back up off the nigh-monochromatic veldt floor. Let's set it back into the sky. Kick rocks, red bishop.

The red-billed firefinch, our bird, my bird, picks up a seed somehow. Birds do this. Oh, all the time. It's a bird thing that happens. I know: I'll *feed* the red-billed firefinch to apologize for murdering it. The bird eats some of these seeds I have for it. By the tree I just pictured. Good bird, good tree, good seeds. It eats some of these seeds, then somehow, drops one or two somewhere else. Maybe it shits the seeds out. Maybe some seeds got lodged in its feathers and finally fall free. There's a plausible explanation for all of this. Certainly more plausible than how a catfish, whole, could wind up on the nigh-monochromatic veldt floor.

The bird, our bird, my red-billed firefinch, when it's not being dead is *quite the flyer* and, there's your seed. Maybe in warm guano, and soon a flower blooms hectares from where it had been. Then, our ancestor encounters it. Now, I'd argue that if the human has seen the flower before and knows that it usually blooms only miles away from this place, that human might experience collage.

Otherwise, they would experience: *Hey, new flower. Right where the flowers are that always bloom here.*

In other words, I think the experience of collage requires that one recognizes two things from different contexts recontextualized into a new, single one. Without recognizing that there was a decontextualization in the process, we might experience juxtaposition. But that's not all collage does.

Humanity's first encounter with collage was a *familiar* flower blooming where none like it had before.

Rather, *I* experience something with collage that's more than juxtaposition—something more transparent in its arrangement, such that the hand behind the new context doesn't get to keep its cutting hush-hush. That's what I'm after when I make work using collage as strategy.

Disruption is a fact of collage. Whether we speak of the hole cut in one context as a part of its decontextualization or our recognition of recontextualization on the other end of the procedure, something is where it wasn't and is doing some new work where it is now.

The seedling breaching the surface of the dirt is a kind of disruption, it's not a disruption of how *this plant works*; neither might we perceive the nigh-monochromatic veldt doing something other than what it does. But, a seedling breaching the hood of a Toyota Sienna? I think for the disruption to be made plain, you mustn't imagine the plant growing smoothly from the minivan's hood. You must recognize evidence of the decontextualization that made this new context. You must notice *the cut*.

Humanity's first encounter with collage was a *familiar* flower from some distant place uprooted, still fresh, found on the ground.

Careful, this feels like the beginning of a narrative. It must resolve into a new context. One in which the veldt is as shifted as the seed. Some of that could be offset by a third element. Consider this here. The veldt —the site—still getting to be a site. All veldtish and whatnot, adorned with an uprooted flower. Such a flower may be a dying flower if it isn't replanted well, and this flower, though uprooted and some considerable distance from home, is still *fresh*.

This takes me back to my earlier formulations—with dead birds (of rhetorical causes and others). Of scenes that suggest foul play. Was death *a third recontextualizing element*? Recognizable as a disruption of the teeming life. A disruption that is not *only* aesthetic—there are lives to consider, but aesthetic, nonetheless—the scene (theater) of the crime is an arrangement of three-dimensional things (composition).

In this sense, the "nature" of the new context becomes operative, a third element at work without needing to cut from a third material source. For that to function in:

> Humanity's first encounter with collage was a *familiar* flower from some distant place uprooted yet still fresh on the ground among local flowers growing in the field.

That's a lot.

If the *where* isn't just the veldt—where flowers could grow—but set amongst flowers growing, is what draws us to see the flower, cut from a field several yonders away, a flash first of a different shape or a different color? Something we don't recognize until we recognize it and, in that instant, collage? A flower—you've seen it before, though hectares from here, hectares back, closer to where there is water. The flower is red as a dead, red bishop. Still the flower is there, uprooted, dying, but still rather fresh, against the blue blooms. Impossible. Those red flowers do not grow here. *It does not go here yet here it goes.* And now this blue-flowering veldt is a veldt with an uprooted red flower. My ancestor demands an explanation. Oh, believe me, my ancestor has a perfectly good capacity for wonder. If they are hunting or foraging—they've left known food sources behind. But, like a catfish on a veldt floor, nigh monochromatic, crashing into a sea of blossoms, my ancestor wants to know how the flower got here.

But before they get to the *how*, they are in the disruption of *what*. And then: *that*.

> Humanity's first encounter with collage was some disruption of their sense of place.

> Humanity *cut* its first encounter with collage when it didn't recognize *how* the disruption occurred.

This uprooted bloom, a long way from home. Almost gone.

I am fascinated by the compressed drama of "Somebody's Calling My Name," and, here, I mean the song as a whole. Though there are as many recorded variations as a tradition of repetition and revision is bound to produce, the consistent declaration "Somebody's calling my name" is a marvel. It links the realm of the physical and spiritual: the speaker needs someone in the physical world to hush so that they might better hear the call simultaneously issuing forth from the supernatural. The speaker straddles life and death and, with the repeated "What shall I do?" seems in a position to make a decision about a physical life (that in a refusal of eternal life is a kind of death) or to choose physical death for eternal life.

Proximity to death, that is to be "almost gone," haunts "Sometimes I Feel like a Motherless Child," a spiritual dating all the way back to the days *Roots* chronicled.

> Sometimes I feel like I'm almost gone
> A long way from home.

Death is close. The absence of references to God in the lyrics of "Sometimes I Feel like a Motherless Child" suggests that *home* might not be a heavenly one. To die "a long way from home" is to die alone among those who may not care for or about your death. If God is in the picture, there's no room for the hopeless sinner who winds up all the way gone, a long way from the presence of the Lord. This seems to be the epistemology of most versions of "Somebody's Calling My Name." Many variations include the line:

Soon one morning, death come creepin' in my room . . .

And follow it up with:

I'm so glad, got me religion on time.

A more recent version recorded by multi-instrumentalist Ry Cooder offers no such relief.

It begins with a command to hush, similar to traditional versions:

You better Hush, hush, hush, hush,

yet the addition of "you better" makes the implicit threat of ordering "hush" explicit.

In Cooder's bleak take, the speaker hears someone—a bedside mourner, not Jesus—calling their name for to *petition* an absentee Jesus on the speaker's behalf:

Somebody's calling my name
Crying oh my Lord, oh my Lord

The drama unfolds around the speaker, reminiscent of Emily Dickinson's "I heard a fly buzz when I died." Where in traditional versions the speaker is ultimately saved, having found religion, Cooder's speaker may die in desperate uncertainty, knowing only that their mother cannot help them.

You can call for your mother
But your mother can't do you no good

Cooder's version posits that sound or silence in the absence of a spiritual realm, both come to Death.

I heard Cooder's first as a sample on X Clan's second album, *Xodus*. The song "Fire and Earth (100% Natural)" juxtaposed the sample with an interpolated intro from the Jimmy Castor Bunch's "Troglodyte." Under that collaged convo, an organ plays "Pop Goes the Weasel" at an awkward, dirgelike tempo. Then a gunshot.

A veldt, a dead fish, bird, uprooted flower? This audio collage, I came to recognize, in the context of the X Clan album, then amplified by the music video, is a dig at white antiblack lies about Blackfolx being primitive. Castor is cut to ventriloquize white racist fantasy (synched in the video to found footage of a white man performing in blackface), naming Black people "Cave Men. Cave Women. Neanderthals. Troglodytes."

Which is to say, calling us out our names.

Recontextualized from the 1986 Cooder take, "You better hush" seemed to me to be telling white people to shut the fuck up or else. After each negative Castor-sampled epithet, we hear the sampled "hush" until the gunshot hushes "Castor," retorting with a corrective "somebody's calling my [real] name." My name. Then the call, Brother J drawling: "Ahhhhhh yeah. Come on come on come on," followed by a back-and-forth routine between J and Professor X: "To the east, my brother, to the east."

What X Clan's usage of the sample, the sample's source, and the sources that the sampled source samples have in common is the arrangement of multiple voices in overlapping cross talk. What draws me to them is the multifarious arc of the word: *Hush*. It is an entreaty, a command, a threat.

In a lawsuit filed in May 2020, members of X Clan stand accused of repeatedly raping Patrice Griffin in 1989. At the time, Griffin was fourteen years old, had run away from home, and was sleeping in the offices of X Clan's organization, the Blackwatch Movement. The two surviving members of X Clan vehemently deny Griffin's allegations.

Who better hush?

Prior to Rutgers's Color Inside the Lines: Visuality and Visibility of Race in Poetry symposium, I asked the convener, Evie Shockley, for a prompt that could guide my remarks. She replied:

> I'm personally interested in whether or in what ways you think of your visual poetics as "black" (as opposed to the subjects you take up in them). OR to what extent you think of your vis poetics as making it less easy to "look away" from the analytical work you're doing, so to speak. (email)

In 2019, I chose the first. I was excited to come get to a closer consideration of "Blackness" as a graphical arrangement of language. Much of what's left of this lecture pursues that thread.

Yet, I think now of the second option, how my visual poetics might "[make] it less easy to 'look away' from the analytical work" my poems do. Shockley, signifying on the lyric from "Dixie," is suggesting more than a reader "looking away" from a critical analysis out of disinterest. "Dixie," a minstrel song that boomed in popularity during the Civil War as an anthem for homesick Confederate Soldiers and the nostalgic folk back home, offers a mode of "looking away" that abets Black subjugation.

Wondering over hushing myself as a performer of loud-assed, colored silences, I am unsure of whether a reader's decision to not *look away* trades on the assumption that they will later be able to *look at* my colored ass reading the poems for them or teaching them how to read them, like demonstrating a new dance.

Shockley's prompts were not mutually exclusive, and I hope I haven't cast them as such. I could, for example, argue that the possibility of surveillable Blackness (option 1) might be what draws the eyes (option 2).

But what's recuperative about the second option is Shockley's focus on the *analytical work* she locates in my poetry's visible *and* visual qualities. As Lee puts it:

> Much of Kearney's work offers . . . performances of improvisation, collision, rupture, and augmentation through an often deliberate performance of excess. . . .
>
> . . . The layers of different typographies reference different periods of time and competing rhetorics. This work refuses to let us ignore the violent erasure and consumption of black bodies across history through the visual layering of language.

This performed excess is a *dintelligible* cross talk.

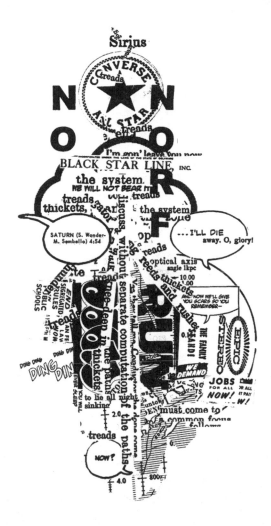

Dintelligibility is a concept I describe thusly:

> a phenomenon where what appears as noise in noise to some (thus, in-
> sensible but perhaps sensual) is in fact complex contrapuntal signals re-
> sulting in a "legible noise," sensible/sensual and sensible through the sen-
> sual and vice versa (sensiual or sensualble or sensiblesual).

If there's a Blackness to the visuality of my visual poetry, it exists not first as a material but as an activity of recognition in dintelligibility.

It's essential to put down that in no sense is this about an essential Blackness. Airea D. Matthews is currently laying shade on that, penning penumbra, umbrage tooken—as one might say—to the bridge and thrown off by way of her searing poem "Making an Essential Nigga." Here, I am reminded of a TV spot from back in the day for the Black femme's lifestyle glossy *Essence*: "Essence is you-ou"—this jingle ran round about the same time as the hoodtastic *Hey Love* slow-jam compilation was in mail-order readiness. "Noooooo my brother, you've got to buy your own," cooed the knoq-off Billy Dee—these two ads dueted to def on BET, bet, between clips on *Video Soul* and *Video Vibrations*. These ads, like Jerry and Aretha's McDLT advert, for us, for us to buy; that is, to buy our own. *That* essence, lower case, is us in so much as any mascon is simultaneously a mask on and a mask off, which is to say, a mascon, or cultural mass concentration (thanks, Stephen Henderson): what we say we recognize when we say we are seeing ourselves seeing ourselves, a.k.a. the nod, the *that's the jam*, the *nahmean*.

A graffitied wall—bombed/tagged/wildstyled/stickered—which is the paradigmatic image from which the previous poem up-jumps—is neither unique nor formally particular to Black social spaces; that such a wall got bombed on due to several factors—some socioeconomic and some aesthetic which, in some cases, includes intentional, strategic, communal participation via a crew of graf writers; that such a wall might exist and might not be painted over because of several *more* factors arranging and extending the initial ones; that such a wall might not only indicate "blight" but signify a teeming excess of signal, the visual equivalent of the raucous-ass knucklehead chorus that is a hip-hop posse cut; that I might recognize such a wall with at least two sets of eyes on that word *recognize* is less about seeing what I figure would be an essentially specious essential Blackness. Rather, it's this rhetorical doubling of *recognize* synesthized and synthesized to an encounter with the page that has me thinking of Black visuality vis-à-vis visibility (and vice versa) as Dr. Shockley proposes them.

I'm saying, the rhetorical construction of *recognize* as applied to the visual field is where I'm housing a working Blackness. That these poems, like the sonic collage productions of DJ Premier, Madlib, or J Dilla, play on the ability to recognize the cut. These artists use samples to make music. An *intertextual and intertextural* music:

> Sampling is after more than the phrase, this is something I think people who don't think much about sampling don't recognize. That those who are sampling are after text *and* texture. And often, they are after a multiplicity of textures that will combine to make a single text.
>
> These textures *must*—and I don't mean this aesthetically, but technically, by which the aesthetic may follow—have different textures because the sources were recorded using different instruments, with different

players, on different mics, in different rooms, using different mixes, made by different engineers, stored on often different media, at often wildly different stylistic eras.

It isn't just about a bass line. It's about all of those differences juxtaposed with other differences and how they hold together or fall apart. It's timbre.

And in that relation of recontextualization, the disruption of the chopped breaks in a composition whose anomalous textures form a new one, we recognize what's happening and nod our heads to the fact that despite all the cuts, it has a pulse.

I want to compose poems that play on the ability to recognize that cut.

But how?

Via texture.

The "Loud-Assed Colored Silence" poems, with their smooth typefaces, might only signal collage through quotation marks or a multiplicity of typefaces. Yet in the act of *retyping* the text I meant to collage, I was not cutting, but quoting. That is, it was not clear that the blooms were *removed* from other fields.

These poems, composed with photoediting software, preserve the textures of the source's letterforms, each poem collaged from dozens of different sources across centuries of printing and scans of wide-ranging resolutions. Then, there's the texture of the cutting itself. Ascenders and descenders clipped, diagonal shearings that cant the typographic baseline, cleavings beneath the x-heights, all of this à la poet Susan Howe's remarkable "Tom Tit Tot" poems from *Debths*. These techniques presence the cut and the act of cutting: meaning my hand's act of cutting isn't in the cut.

Thus, these poems, like the sample-based composition "Workinonit" from J Dilla's *Donuts*, are textual and textural composites, pieces that decenter a fleshy, lyric voice, but distribute my voice through the constellated layers and interruptions, proximities and nubbings, the dintelligible frequencies of optical utterance the reader is called to recognize.

Recognize: as in *know again* and as in *acknowledge* and here I want to resist a primary and secondary ordinance as sequenced in the dictionary, that uh 1 and uh 2. Rather, I am thinking of a simultaneity similar to what I think gets activated in South Central LA vernacular: *You better recognize.* Which stages *recognition* as *acknowledging what you already know again lest it teach you what you should know you know.*

In this way, it favors the older "Hush. Hush," by way of "You better hush." An admonishment for silence to allow for recognition of what's known. The song's speaker commands—"Hush. Hush. Somebody's calling my name." In that song, there is death in what may or may not be recognized. But the act of attending is what we attend to in the lyric's opening.

You better *hush.* That command lies in the cut of *You better recognize.* For the *You better* (and the insistent *hush*) is, in its structure, a sideways threat, even when uttered in play. Recognizing, in its activity, is *a reading of a context* and an understanding of the conditions that compose it lest shit go sideways. This relates to "mess," which I've written about before as a liminal space—the passage between Order and Garbage.

That *sign* in *sign*ify, that is semiotic, but also conjures semiauto, like a tag is a gang sign on a street sign that tells you whose streets these aren't even as they put names all up in the street. You better recognize. When I see it, that *inessence*, I recognize I am there and not there—it isn't me, it isn't my own—but it is temporary, transitional.

A graffitied wall is a mess. Thus it isn't, in essence, Blackness. But Blackfolx the shit at recognizing the message in that shit. The signal in that noise.

So, to get to Dr. Shockley's prompt, CPT-like: what's the Blackness in the visibility and visuality in my work? I want to press toward approaching Black recognizing's activity, that is that it isn't uh 1 and uh 2, but that in my now work, visibility and visuality might be simultaneous: *e.g.*, looking at how I stay looking at what I'm looking at.

This process, for me, activates a poetics I recognize as consonant with a long-term, sometimes ironic investigation of the condition of having context mainly through forced recontextualization. I mean to understand a Black existential reality by way of an aesthetic process. I mean to engage strategies concentrated in Black compositional traditions and their attendant institutions—the COGIC choir's floating stanzas, the cutting session, the crew's overtalking and boom boxes, the corner's diegetic intersection, the meeting *after* the faculty meeting, the war council playing a voicemail on speakerphone, the salon (hair).

Also? This shit slaps.

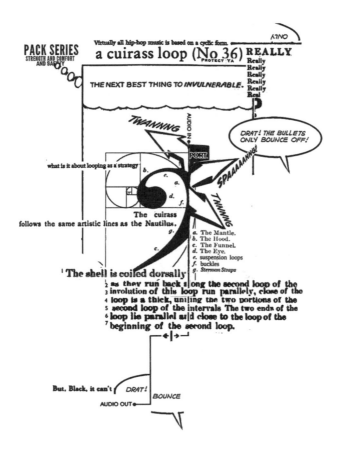

"But Black, It Can't—" is the first of a series of speculative fiction poems. The project's framework: each would be a piece of rhetorical sonic armor drawn from a genre of Afro-diasporic music. "But Black, It Can't," like similar collaged poems, developed as a series of relational activities and recognitions.

The seed of the poem is a quote from an interview of the hip-hop producer 9th Wonder, published in the now defunct magazine *Scratch* back in 2005. 9th had a rep as a throwback-style producer, hearkening to boom bap associated with folk who might consider themselves "true school" hip-hop heads but would be called "backpackers" derisively for their associations with geeky, college fan bases and their requisite Jan-Sports. 9th famously used a software platform called Frooty Loops for his beatmaking, the loop being the basic form of sample-based (so called "real") hip-hop. In the interview, 9th stated: "Every producer should flip 'Nautilus' by Bob James. It's a rite of passage." I've freighted this quote in my mental crate for a hot minute, usually using it as a route by which to track the roots of the distinction between loop-based and chop-based hip-hop production.

Listen to the first minute or so of the original.

Then, consider the RZA, the abbot of the Wu-Tang Clan, who looped a sample of "Nautilus" for Ghostface Killah's "Daytona 500" from his album *Ironman*.

And finally, check out 9th Wonder himself, who chopped up "Nautilus" for the title track for his second collabo with LA emcee Murs, "Murray's Revenge."

Now: "Nautilus" is a mellow-ass fusion instrumental. A nautilus is a mollusk. Its shell is on its back, protecting its softer innards. Armor mounted like a backpack.

In investigating the anatomy of nautiluses, I found that their intestines are sometimes described as *loops*. I looked up "nautilus," "anatomy," and "loop" and found a nineteenth-century text I proceeded to chop and collage.

The poem was shifting, in part because I was changing my mind about how I was going to do what I was going to do, but also because the resources I found—even the ones I decided not to use—were reshaping my sense of what the poem could say.

34

Specifically: I was back and forth with myself about how many pictures of objects versus pictures of words would be up in this piece.

The armor series *wants* at some level to be indexical. "This is a shield. This is a helmet. This is a codpiece." I wanted to do this without pictures of the same. I opted, at that moment, to remain constrained with symbols that are "typographic."

The bass clef "rhymes" with the shell of a nautilus, its curve and synecdochic spiral begin the eye's trip while still "reading" as a symbol meaning: *hear bass*, a significant component of hip-hop music. Associative success, but I felt I needed something else to amplify the visual pun: bass clef equals nautilus shell. So I included *the golden section*. The golden section diagrams an abstract concept of purported visual pleasure; as a kind of formula, it felt less like an illustration to me than a reduction of a shell, plus nautilus shells and the section have been associated in the past—this tracked. The intestinal loop text, bass clef, and golden section became the center of the poem.

I began to add more and more. Accretion becomes a factor as added textual elements create new or deepened associations and increased intertextual crosscuts. What was a nonce idea becomes a "head"—a motif, as it might in an improvisational musical performance. Similarly, here, I'm working to attend to possibilities, to perceive. Sometimes, I know the precise phrase that will chime with part of the composition. But the poem's textuality is not centralized. It's communal and relational. Which means, in the case of this poem, I didn't know I had anything *for sure* until I was maybe 75 percent in. And that instant came with a moment of improvisation and association.

"Backpacks" had proven too complicated to work into the poem without a visual referent (at one point, I had little straps and buckles stuck on letters. Trust: this is better). So, I decided to just name a piece of armor. It was difficult to find a part of armor designed solely for the warrior's back. That would suggest they ran away from battle! So I settled on *cuirass*. Returning to the lexical motif that had anchored the poem, "loop," I searched "cuirass" and "loop" and found this.

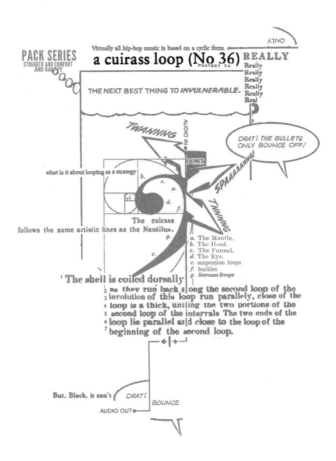

You don't seem excited.

This is what makes the poem work!

"Cuirass Loop No. 36" is from a book of military history, more specifically about the Roman invasion of Britain.

"Cuirass Loop No. 36" uprooted from that book, floating without context does little.

But recontextualized into the veldt of this poem, "36" alludes to the Wu-Tang Clan's first album, *Enter the 36 Chambers*. That album is part of a narrative framing an East Coast hardcore corrective to G-Funk's early '90s dominance. Thus, *Enter the 36 Chambers* is a totem of so-called "true school" hip-hop.

It's a backpacker's grail.

And its big, raucous posse cut?

"Protect ya neck."

A call for armor.

You better recognize.

Yet how does this tie to silence?

If I don't *hush* and instead fix to voice these poems with my flesh, my throat's small lexicon of timbres, my diaphragm's limited air, my head's slow calibrations, the spit that sputters pronunciation—all these would natter and chatter, talking over the poem's call.

Hush.

My body would make the poem unrecognizable. *I* would become something to *look at* as a means to *look away* from what the poem is there to show you. And, in all that loud-assed business, I, too, would be unable to hear the call, so afraid of a physical silence that may actually stave off a kind of death.

Hush.

I am sick of being a specious prosthetic mouth, a grotesque one with impossibly swollen lips, swollen as if struck or drawn to look struck. Struck with what? A fist, a grease pencil, a peculiar idea: that I am a caveman with no language. I might just be a pair of lips on a pair of legs; legs that know the latest dances; legs with feets that don't fail; strong legs for to support the toting of bales.

Hush.

I get tired, sometimes, of speaking. I open my mouth, the words skitter out in zippy preposterosities, eloquintessences, electrolocutions; words so big they gape my massive shit-talking mouth, emerging slick with my spit. That ancient elixir, articulation's sweat, my puckers all tuckered. And wearied, I turn to moan some, but with the thick ribbons what's my lips, it sounds like someone's Christmas.

What shall I do? What shall I do?

You better hush.

"We should heed that 'GET AWAY.'"

#WEREWOLFGOALS

For Marcia Kearney, Nicole McJamerson, CAConrad,
Ron Edwards, torrin a. greathouse, and Justin Phillip Reed

A note before beginning in earnest

I have capitulated to an etymological inequity. Werewolf *is a gendered term. The Old English* wer *means "man," and* wulf, *"wolf."* Lycanthrope *is drawn from* Lycaon, *an Arcadian cannibal king who tried tricking Zeus into eating people. Angered, Zeus turned Lycaon into a wolf. Lykos, "wolf." Ly- canthrope.* Lykos *and* anthros*—"man." Though any person, it seems, can become a werewolf, most examples I've read about or seen depicted are men. I will use* person *and* wolf *later. This may mark a failure of language.*

Lycanthropy is a "disorder" in which someone believes they are a were- wolf. When I use the term "lycanthropy" and its variations, I do so, as many others have, to denote the actual state of being a werewolf.

43

We must begin with an understanding.

This lecture is about writing and werewolf practice.

In writing "writing and werewolf practice," I do not speak in figures. No *like* or *as* haunts, invisibly, the phrase, grinning.

Writing's no *proxy*, here, for a werewolf practice; neither do I aspire to write my way toward something *werewolf-like*.

So, while I will talk about writing, mostly I will discuss years of desire to be a werewolf.

It's best I set down that before poetry I was committed to a werewolf métier. I've tried to recollect my introduction to the subject. This has proven fruitless, and I resist the urge to speculate for fear that I'd invent something too apt for this lecture. Better I say I can't recall *not* knowing about werewolves and, simultaneously, being drawn to them. In werewolves, I do not see *kin*: I know I am not one. I see a goal of sorts.

To this end, before I'd turned ten, I worked out a regimen of exercises from cinematic werewolf metamorphosis scenes. The idea was to condition my body, for to prepare and, if I'm honest, *activate* my own transformation.

Stretches to accommodate a wolf/person anatomy, meditative sensory reallocation to facilitate my new perceptual enhancements, vigorous trials of focus . . . It remains true that I hope flexing my hand until the palm is convex while curling my fingers into hooked right angles will *produce* claws. It's more than a tensorial curve, but a *pushing* you must picture. Conjure a knuckle there you've forgotten.

When I dream, sometimes I've dreamt myself a werewolf or some other shapeshifter. Only, that's not why I'm talking about my dreams right now.

In some dreams, I am capable of something not quite flight, but if I jump, then rotate my arms just so, against gravity's pull, I suppose, I can forestall alighting, extending the leap's distance, remaining aloft in hung time. I've done this, again and again, such that I know how to manage it in different dreams. What's more, walking around awake or, here, typing as I am and seated, I remember the feeling in my muscles, can remember it as sharply as I recall doing the Shoot, strapping tight Velcro shoes, tearing open Fun Dip with my teeth.

The memory, the sensation of it, seems tied to place and context. I cannot do a backflip except underwater. But I know the sensation and how to achieve it even when I haven't been submerged for more than a year. Even here in this flimsy air, my body remembers, pieces together what it's done.

While stretching my hands into claws, I hunt my memory. Have I ever *felt* talons grow from my fingertips? Do I know the twinge of lupine hair breaking my burning, blossoming skin? How does the paradigm of meaning-making shift when I find I can smell more keenly than I can see? In all these years, have I come closer to knowing?

You might suggest I use writing to account for these questions. Documenting my thoughts about them in a field journal—"May 26: I think I smelled a pig at one mile today." Nope. I've no werewolf archive. There are a few poems, sure; yet they skin the lycanthrope to cover and do some other thing. Those poems, they are not telling you what I am telling you: that I have meant to be a werewolf, and that this has been, I'm afraid, a quiet, lifelong ambition, a discipline I've maintained longer and to less purpose, it would seem, than nearly all else.

45

Still, "less purpose" does not mean no purpose at all. Writing this lecture dogged me to ponder the why of it. Many familiar with my poems could observe that popular associations between werewolves and violence may find chime with my work's steady study of brutality. As is true for many people, violence has been my grim companion. Systemic and personal. With me as subject and object. The werewolf's ability to savage often comes bound to an act of violence visited upon them. An animal attack. A curse. A punishment.

Most of my life, I've found violence inextricable from control. You've a temper you couldn't manage. You force someone do something they don't want to do. You lost in one place and will damn sure "win" in another. Control, absent and present, knotted with violence.

People use the werewolf, my wife—a lifelong horror fiction enthusiast and writer—reminds me, to narrate about control and the social toll of losing it. It should not surprise anyone familiar with my work that control—formal, rhetorical, prosodic, compositional, thematic, performative, and social—are central concerns.

But is this relationship to control why I have wanted to become a werewolf?

In *Shapeshifters: A History*, author John B. Kachuba writes:

The werewolf is probably the most well-known shapeshifter and is the quintessential example of what can go wrong when that animal nature takes control. Its popularity and attraction may say something about our own latent desires to be free of the shackles of morality and social mores and to run naked through the night-time woods, howling at the Moon.

Stephen King, in his unofficial dissertation on horror, *Danse Macabre*, has it:

What we're talking about here, at its most basic level, is the old conflict between id and superego, the free will to do evil or to deny it ... or in Stevenson's own terms, the conflict between mortification and gratification. This old struggle is the cornerstone of Christianity.

The Stevenson he's speaking on is Robert Louis, author of what King considers the foundational werewolf text of popular imagination, *The Strange Case of Dr. Jekyll and Mr. Hyde* (1886). What I find interesting about both Kachuba and King's assessments of werewolfery is a suggestion that by turning into a wolf or wolflike creature, one escapes societal controls. This seems mighty—something or other. Consider Gévaudan, a now gone southern region of France, which from 1764–1767 was beset by a beast many cried was werewolf. Slaughtered about one hundred locals, several savagely decapitated. In answer, King Louis XV sent his royal gunbearer who, with his nephew, slew a 130 lb. wolf who fit a fuzzy description. A couple of months later, the killings continued. Whoops. Karl Hans-Taake, who wrote *The Gévaudan Tragedy: The Disastrous Campaign of a Deported 'Beast,'* notes that "from 1764 to 1767, more than a hundred wolves were killed in Gévaudan. Half a dozen of these wolves were thought to be the Beast."

What I mean to mean with this is that, if one were to become a wolf, free themselves of some shackles, and do evil, there would soon come mobs killing anything what might *remotely* match a lupine profile. This isn't impunity round my woods' neck. One must imagine themselves perceived innocent when in human skin to think so.

White was the word. Mighty white.

Even potential anonymity is contingent. In most of the folklore I'd read, a trope that sticks is injuries a werewolf sustains in either form

47

carries over to the other. Lose a hand? You become a wolf sans paw. Sustain a slash across your muzzle, you wake to a gouged nose in the bathroom mirror.

No. The werewolf as beast or fictional half-person/half-beast was not free of any control I didn't ultimately feel subject to. An alibi means nothing if no one de-escalates before firing that silver bullet.

What the werewolf has that *I* want is a transformed relationship between body and place, this by way of their keener senses. They would know things about themselves in their surroundings I never could.

I stand sometimes, in a stiff wind, sniffing, listening. I peer in the darkness trying to understand what shapes light doesn't see.

I think, too, of werewolves' powerful musculature, I imagine it coupled with my new senses, enhancing my proprioception—"perception or awareness of the position and movement of the body," allowing me to take joy in motion through space, instead of fear. Is that freedom from *morality*? Whose? And is its fleetingness *freedom* at all? Contingent upon when the pale moon comes to shine its face on me?

This would be a time to know better the briar's signal and noise. That this knowing could become part of my body's memory, not as a dream but as a passage of conscious time, astonishes me.

Monstrous strength to fight those who harm me? Sure.

But when I dream of revenge, I'm not proud to say, I don't care for ambiguity about my identity.

Later for a mask of fur and fangs.

I sit at my desk, my fingers hunt and peck over keys. I never mastered typing by touch. I stare down, almost at the letters, they stare back, gamely. It's fine. It goes on like this until it doesn't. I'm not certain when it happens, the shift, when I stop *seeing* the keys. Then, there, I go not by touch, but by a flickering spatial memory—my fingers, I guess, still pouncing, not sliding. And for a pass, I am somewhere else, there in the hippocampus, a part of the brain that shares a name with a half-horse/half-fish I learned about as a child studying mythical creatures. Hippocampus: a seahorse-shaped curve of the brain where there be episodic memory.

When I'm in the hippocampus, is it that the letters on the butterfly keyboard are no longer those designed by Apple, but are *my* L, my E, my T, R, and S—somehow both shapeless and contoured, there along the limbic's dark cliff? Both in the semantic sequence what spells "LETTERS" and the QWERTY thicket undoing it. My fingers stalk, quickly.

Next, what happens? I catch myself thinking: *did I stroke the T without looking?* Whatever swifter animal my index had become downshifts human, as if its sense of smell dims. I tap the T, maybe. But perhaps the Y. Close. I assess. *You almost know*, I go. Almost.

I wonder in the moments that follow about the relationship between spatial memory and what many name *muscle memory*. In suggesting muscles' ability to remember, I didn't know to distinguish the growth of myonuclei, the cells in muscles' fiber and the neurons in the motor cortex. Memory in the fiber makes it easier for muscle to return, even after atrophy from lack of use. The motor cortex, with its network of connections, accounts for the series of movements that become reflexive after practice.

Flexing my hands, again, into their blunt series of angles, I stare at them. Nothing in the place where the claws should be. What is it I'm teaching them to remember? To know?

Public education in Pasadena, California, being what it was, I'd no choice in lycanthropy but self-education. Loups-garous-ji-chagulia. Means for locating accredited training, or even after-school programs, were scant and unhelpful. The yellow pages skipped "Werewolf" altogether. Further, unlike most of my interests, including poetry, puppetry, and drawing, lycanthropy remained an unknown passion to my parents. My brother had an inkling. When I was nine and he thirteen, I told him I learned a spell meant to shift my shape. Found it in a library book called *Black Magic, White Magic*. I remember it, even now.

> I will go into a cat
> With sorrow, a sigh, and a black shot.
> And I will go in the devil's name,
> Aye while I come home again.

Immediately, my brother laid out the theological problem of a Lutheran doing anything in "the devil's name."

There were other hitches. In addition to the spell's verbal component, an unidentified ointment or salve was required. And what *was* set down in black and white was hermeneutic trouble. The final line's euphemistic "home" in proximity to "the devil" is *dangerously* ambiguous. I hadn't a clue what a "black shot" was; "with sorrow, a sigh" profess a bleakness the propulsive meter belies. And then, of course, I would be going "into a cat."

Reckon I objected to species? Natch, cats aren't wolves. Even so, I respected progression. I was in fourth grade. I had been in third grade, briefly, a Cub Scout. Wolf badge followed Bobcat. I'd work my way up.

Was it aesthetic? The spell's prosody of tight, often internal slant rhyme (cat/shot, will/while, name/come/home), assonance (cat/black, I/sigh/aye/while/I), and stressed to unstressed rhyme (go/sorrow and will/devil) still goes into my poetics.

No. In truth, my issue with the spell was grammatic. The preposition was wrong.

What I've come to understand is that the demonstrative nature of were-wolves, which is to say their *externalized* transformation from person to not only person, is articulated most simply in prepositions.

Should we take *person* and *wolf* as potential syntactic subjects, we have the start of our werewolf logistic. It's best we remember that a werewolf isn't a werewolf when they are hairy and clawed. They are a werewolf *because* they must turn hairy and clawed. The metamorphosis, then, is not *becoming a werewolf*. It is a *demonstration* of their lycanthropic nature, often commanded without any agency on the werewolf's part. Now: these constraints[1] are specific and not intended as metaphor. While becoming a werewolf *may* involve agency (via a spell, consensual exposure, or years and years and years of devoted practice), until one is no longer a werewolf, the compulsory shapeshifting the werewolf undergoes is not an apparatus of state law, cultural convention, or cooperation even under duress.

Next, I wish to offer that the end of the transformation indicates an *optical demonstration* of the werewolf logistic. It is not a *culmination* of lycanthropy itself, but a demonstration of its presence. So: when I use

---

1. I resisted the term "conditions" because of its ableist connotations; but it's very important that I be understood here. I am not using the werewolf as a vehicle for any other identity or subject position. I am a cisgendered, heterosexual Black man. I want to be a werewolf, too.

the terms *demonstration* or *optical demonstration*, I only mean to mean that an event of external metamorphosis is complete.

Finally, I'll capitulate to a presumptive topological aspect of most Western lycanthropic relationships: that lycanthropy happens *to people*. I apologize for this limit to my knowledge. After all, lupine communication *is* an established fact. Should wolves share a cultural understanding of werewolves, perhaps their lore has it as a thing people visit upon their packs.

At any rate, after initial contact (in the case of biological lycanthropic spread), the relationship between wolf and person is proprioceptive. Their spatial tension structures the modes of metamorphosis under analysis here, thus the insertion of a preposition between *person* and *wolf*.

Person *into* wolf: The person moves to occupy the body of the wolf. Such an arrangement may require the presence of an actual wolf that becomes a vehicle for some aspect/component of the person. This is the cat spell. I didn't want to go *into* a cat *or* wolf, for that matter. The werewolf was no sinewy, shaggy suit to wear. Such an arrangement described a separation between me and the wolf; I meant to be *one thing*. It's possible to imagine *into* as the person's body producing a wolf body in its place (*into*, here, takes on the sense of composition, not place-ment). But the ambiguity's too slippery.

Into Exercise: Focus on the idea of a suppository—a narrow, tapering shape that dissolves—the same color you imagine yourself to be.

Or, using muscles only, compress your body into a suppository shape. Dissolution will come.

Wolf *inside* **person**: The beast-within arrangement. The person is an ambulatory kennel or pregnant with a more or less mature wolf. The wolf shelters/gestates there, waiting to emerge.

Inside Exercise: Fix in your mind an idea of a small thing getting big-ger—it could be an object or sound, an odor or memory. It can grow as large as you imagine yourself as a place to be. Then, it must grow some-what larger with you still there to imagine it.

Or open wide your mouth and tense your esophageal tract in an ex-pulsive attitude. If possible, run your fingers down your sternum, feeling for the latch.

Wolf *with* person or person *with* wolf: A conjunction—*and*—could be better, but *with* more expressly suggests collaboration and amplification. Prepositions, also, seem to me to imply activity in a spatial context, necessary in the case of metamorphosis into optical demonstration. The relation re: person/wolf seems one of physical separateness but bound through some other intimacy; or, perhaps one serving as an appendage to the other.

> *<u>With</u> Exercise: Go low to the ground and move in a circle, inhaling deeply for to smell your own motion. You may do this all with any form of assistance or via visualization.*

Person *by* wolf or wolf *by* person: Where *with* presents an intangible connection regardless of proximity, *by* denotes an *adjacent* nearness, though there stands, also, a connotation of support. The-one-*by*-the-one, their separateness seems foregrounded (relational language of *with* intimates a movement toward union, distinct from "standing by" someone). *By* may also indicate authorship—that the respective person or wolf has *composed* the respective wolf or person. This makes *by* compelling.

> *By Exercise: Think on falling, but in this thought be caught by what you call* wolf *that you catch, too, as it catches you. Maws? Arms? Paws? Palms? A lap? A back?*
>
> *Or on a moonlit night, lean sideways far as you can without falling. Wait a spell. Or fold your fingers to the middle knuckles, knead these makeshift paws against your flesh.*

Person *against* wolf or wolf *against* person: Our pair are separate though, here, in vexed contact. The person and wolf touching each other, close. Like *with* and *by*, *against* introduces affinity—by way of its absence. The wolf and person are in conflict. Over what? Generically, recall, control.

> *Against Exercise: I am against an against relation, thus against against exercises. A conundrum.*

Wolf *up* person: Who acts here? Who has thrust wolf up person? Agency and balance are at odds in this arrangement. *Up* used this way has a vernacular denotation of violent action (to go up someone's head)—is this the aforementioned curse, the *punitive* werewolf logistic? In excess of *up*'s dynamic activity, the lycanthropic *up* is also a preposition of verticality. Wolf lodged high up person, difficult to reach.

> <u>*Up*</u> *Exercise: If you get on your hands, your knees? If you then breathe out, making your spine a convex line tucking your bottom jaw in toward your sternum? If you, finally, breathe in, invert your back, and cast your gaze upward? What?*
>
> *And if not, imagine something not you, buried in you, that part of you is above it, as the sky—you've been told—is above you and was above the thing buried in you, even before it was buried there?*

Wolf *down* person[2]: How like *up* that it troubles balance. Dominant US culture has prepared us for a *down* werewolf logistic with its morguefuls of dead metaphors associating sublimation or repression with depths. Feeling down? A trauma deep down inside? You note how quickly we can rhyme associations of "down" with pathology? The wolf, here, is *down* there, and it was driven or has dug itself in, like *up*, to resist contact. Beyond optical demonstration, which does not require equity, *down* can bring to bear a sense of social abjection.

> <u>Down</u> *Exercise: A thought exercise. Inside a relation which includes outsiding, you are the outside inside of which goes what others cast out. What is outside to you, being as you are, inside as out?*
>
> *Or:*
>
> *Be as still as* you *consider still. Do not think* wolf *any more than* you *think* person. *Slowly, deliberately engage your core muscles as if to shit backwards.*

2. There is also the eating pun. This slurs the wolf.

Person *under* wolf or wolf *under* person: Let's acknowledge the verticalist inequity from jump, yes? Even bearing that cultural, rhetorical order, I mean to be less figurative; one needs be so with lycanthropy: the teeth are real, the fur, the claws, of course. One physically under one as *a fluid formation* need not be a re-rehearsal of domination. If a horse and its rider could exchange roles at different points of a journey, for example.

> *Under Exercise: Push-ups with additional weight strapped to one's back, if manageable, make a good preparation. Do not, however, push your body* away *from the floor, but imagine you are pressing the floor* away *from your body. In fact, focusing thusly may be more effective than doing push-ups at all, whether or not you lie down prone on any surface.*

Wolf *from* person: *From* is tricky—the wolf is composed of the person's material—thus two separate species exist in a remixed union. This is similar to *by* (in the sense of authorship), sans the person's implicit agency and shared flesh. *From* may also suggest the person is the wolf's point of origin, making it not unlike the *inside* logistic. Though, as I hope is clear, the connotative associations of each preposition's multiple meanings are difficult to extract. And isolate. Finally, in *from* lurks a Victorian expulsive urge.

> *From* Exercise: *Massage, have massaged, or imagine massaged the region round your mouth and nose, gently drawing them forward. Patience.*

I could go on. And am tempted to do so. Prepositions are key to indicating a point of tension in space, particularly between two nouns whose dynamic relationship is fraught—who is subject, who is object, who makes it so, who preserves the relation?

Person *through* wolf—a passage or an achievement?

Wolf *till* person—an emphasis on the constraint of time; that soon come full moon rising.

Person *along* wolf. Person *at* wolf. Are they in conflict? Accord? On all fours? Rampant? Showing belly?

Who runs person *to* wolf?

VISUALIZING PREPOSITIONS:
WEREWOLF METAMORPHOSIS SEQUENCES

I suspect that none of the werewolf metamorphoses I've seen in films would be credibly considered documentaries. They do, though, remind me of the televisual true crime trope of *dramatic reenactment*, in that I would argue that attempts to render credible scenes of lycanthropic transformation are, in part, forensic efforts. Why? They are speculative while reverse engineering sources of "evidence." The "evidence" in the film? The werewolf at optical demonstration. Or, as popularly called: the werewolf.

Speculation lets subjectivity in, and, as such, the *staging* and *choreography* of the transformation illustrate a feeling toward lycanthropy, an interpretation of it as a relation between person and wolf.

Prepositions provide a linguistic index for these swirling agons of control, tension, and cooperation. Without a verb, prepositions still imply action while leaving the nature of that action in a space of generative ambiguity, which is to say, the preposition can give us a schematic sense (position), a kinetic one (motion and direction), and maybe even an attitude the schema and movement take. Prepositions create a contextual space and a knowing about bodies in that space (proprioception).

But whether the wolf *tears* its way *up* the person or *hunts, whines, leaps* is not this writer's concern. This writer, today, eschews an image-driven vividness for something I think of as the prepositions' more mythic vividness—we are given a thing to *understand* that doesn't *first* rely on simulating Western sensate sense-making. And in the culture from which I first learned about werewolves, that Western sensate sense-making is counterfeitly synonymous with *person*.

Mighty . . . something.

Forgoing the image in that order then prompts me to believe we receive something we do not completely perceive. And, here, I depart, aesthetically, from the films I will discuss, which, driven to depict special effects mastery and make plausible their tack on werewolf transformation, linger over details and propose biological hypotheticals.

Visual media do not default to revealing what a preposition may enshroud. Much can happen out of frame, behind props, or betwixt cuts. In this way, the visual can emphasize what's unseen in ways other media cannot. Visual depictions of werewolf transformations are not opposite to the textual preposition. Rather, the visual may articulate, and in some cases—hyperarticulate—the logistic of the prepositional myth. The filmed metamorphosis is the dream the filmmaker has of the prepositional relation, filtered through the practical possibilities of special effects, budget, Motion Picture Association ratings, and the crew of collaborators. It's a projected reading.

The three films I'll be discussing are from the early '80s—not because I believe this was the best time for werewolf films but because this time was coeval with my burgeoning interest in myth and werewolves. I can only recall seeing one of the films—a short—in full, and it is possible regarding another, I had only animated a still in my imagination. Still, images of the transformations have stuck with me since childhood. There in the part of my head where myths come from, remixed and blurred with where I find me now, what I've learned and misheard before. My poems share that space.

Angela Carter and Neil Jordan's script for *The Company of Wolves* emerges from a similar space, the libidinal swelter of "Little Red Riding Hood," a French fairy tale. Under Jordan's direction, we see wolves obliterate the bodies they share with their human hosts in two striking transformations, both fever dreaming the brutal eros of the Wolf *inside* Person relation. I only remembered one prior to YouTube fact-checking.

The metamorphosis I didn't remember is pretty great, though. The werewolf, named the Young Groom and played by Stephen Rea, tears his human skin from his face in bloody strips, revealing the red, striated musculature beneath. It looks and sounds painful. The fangs are already there, and the puppet head looks not quite people even before the nose and mouth thrust into muzzle.

My scene, however, involves a person's head and face. What I remembered: a white man's mouth forced open as a fully formed wolf's snout thrusts out its gape. Slick, not with blood but saliva. This werewolf—the Huntsman (Micha Bergese)—was a man what swallowed a wolf or had one grown in him. The Huntsman isn't stoic through any of this; he rages in pain. It's difficult to tell whether his agony comes from the metamorphosis or a shotgun wound; Sarah Patterson as Rosaleen (imagine the red flower) had just bucked his arm.

Reviewing the scene after thirty-odd years, I note two things. One: the wolf doesn't climb all the way out of the man's head as I misremembered. The wolf finishes its exit splitting the man's back, like the Hulk splits Bruce Banner's shirts. Two: the wolf presents as a mundane wolf—*Canis lupus*. Yet, the image of the wolf's mouth emerging from the sheath of the Huntsman's mouth draws my attention to maws: the Huntsman "love[s] the company of wolves" and threatens Rosaleen ("All the better to *eat* you with"), after demanding and receiving her promised kiss. It's all about that mouth and the big teeth in it—his my-oh-my-what-long-tongue lolls from his lips, the lupine becoming a visual language the filmmakers wager will be at once strange and familiar.

THRILLER (1983)

This simultaneous uncanniness and mundanity reminds me of the "perilous flux" Margo Jefferson uses to describe Michael Jackson's constant engagement with shapeshifting in his music videos, cosmetic surgeries, the polyglot lexicon of his performance. Jefferson writes:

His appearance is always in perilous flux. Time and again in his videos we see Michael undergoing monstrous transformations: from sweet young man to ghoul (*Thriller*); from natty pop star to black cat (*Billie Jean*); from dancing white-robed shaman to hooligan smashing windows, then seizing and stroking his penis (*Black or White*); from raging hooligan to Buddha (*Scream*). He loves genres that emphasize mutable identities, carefree cartoons and horror tales.

I saw Michael Jackson's *Thriller* video before *The Company of Wolves*. *Thriller* features a protracted transformation scene.

About that transformation. *Thriller* reunited the team of John Landis (director) and Rick Baker (special makeup effects), of *An American Werewolf in London* (1981). *Thriller*'s near fourteen-minute music video as short film was a mythmaking bid sparing no expense. Jefferson writes:

> When people praise Michael Jackson . . . they always mention the 1983 *Thriller* video. That's because it's a short masterpiece, a perfectly thought-through and executed horror tale. It is the tale of the double, the man with two selves and two souls, like Dr. Jekyll and Mr. Hyde. . . . Which is his true self?

To this she adds: "Why does he feel a connection to this dreadful menacing other?"

Jackson's shapeshifting optical demonstration, like many in the genre, including *The Company of Wolves*, forces the onscreen onlooker, so often written to be a woman, to stand watching, screaming, and, importantly, not getting a head start on escaping. Ola Ray does this work gamely as Jackson's letterman-jacketed BMOC jackknifes into the loup-garou stomach cramp. After a series of what sound like MJ's "soul hiccups," he roars: "GET AWAY!" Is that the last bit of Jackson as Jekyll? Prior to the Hyde he was hiding? Maybe? Who was it took Ray out on a full moon night knowing the nature of his "condition"? The car breaking down may have stranded them, but darkness had already fallen. Perhaps he reckoned his prepositional relation as person *over* cat. Person on top, a dom. Still *over* could also suggest a cover-up, like the letterman jacket that doesn't get jacked up in the shift of cat *over* person.

And yes, *cat*. Not wolf. Soon come.

After watching the premiere as everyone else I knew did, I didn't watch the transformation *itself* again for some time. It scared the shit out of me. And of the monster himself? The *Thriller* were-creature is a were-cat/were-cad—Baker wasn't interested in doing another werewolf. Happily, its fur was not Jheri curled, though by rights, some of it should have been.

Baker renders the transformation with a forensic attention to detail. The whiskers piercing the flesh of Jackson's face is my secondmost memory, in a dead heat with the claws making their wet sounds through fingertips that would, in later clips, rock medical tape. Once stuck in the middle of the metamorphosis's grip, pain follows horror for Jackson's unnamed high schooler. But if the transformation in progress isn't agonizing, neither does Jackson appear to take pleasure in it. The bright yellow, feline contacts gogging his eyes along with the FX oral prosthetics make it hard to suss out much beyond gaping shock. Let's consider this an intended effect and not a concession in production or performance. When Jackson looks at his transformed palm, a now cat-man without a mirror, he seeks the only recognition he can get beyond Ray's screaming.

I'm not like other guys. I'm different.

The most important moment of this metamorphosis for me, the signature image locked in my myth brain is the reveal of the transformation's first phase. Michael's mouth a drawerful of cutlery, his eyes like lanterns. His oft buttery lilt turned a guttural-bellowing "GET AWAY!"

We should heed that "GET AWAY."

We learn later, in the video's waking-nightmare structure, I mean, that Jackson is always the were-cat. The ending image, his grinning face, marked only by the feline contacts and haunted by Vincent Price's graveyard cackle, is mere punctuation. His pretty cruelties drive the video more than his dancing.

Decontextualized, "GET AWAY" could be a victim's language. Ola Ray could say it. It seems likely we are *meant* to understand Jackson's character as protecting her. "GET AWAY." If so, who is saying it? The guy who led Ola Ray into the woods *knowing* he was a were-cat. Different.

Not like other guys. Or the fanged one who knows what's coming. "GET AWAY!" "GET AWAY" could be petulant. He says it right after Ray presses to see why he doubles over. *Don't look at me when I'm like this!* "GET AWAY" rhymes with "get out." But it's too late to do either now.

Jackson, sources report, adored horror. Though Landis also says that Jackson found many of the images from fright flicks that Rick Baker showed him "'too scary.'"

AN AMERICAN WEREWOLF IN LONDON (1981)

Did Jackson see *An American Werewolf in London*? Assuredly. Landis and Baker awaited him there as they did me. But in the film, they had not the world's biggest pop star to act as *person* in their werewolf logistic, but David Naughton as David Kessler. Kessler is befuddled by his new reality and often droll about it. Though his first transformation is a clear torment.

Baker's visual effects are here the closest to what I mean by forensic. The focus is on Naughton. There is no one screaming or no onscreen scientist observing. Just us in the dark and Kessler, alone in his lover's brightly lit living room. Struck suddenly by a spike in body temperature, Kessler tears off his clothes. Nothing occludes our examination. For about two and a half minutes, the camera takes him in, studying. Landis says:

> My inspiration was the old 1940s horror movie *The Wolf Man*, starring Lon Chaney, in which—unusually—the werewolf was portrayed as a victim. Films tended to show the transformation from man to wolf through dissolves, but I wanted to capture how painful the entire process would be—and make it painful to watch.

Thus, we inspect the metamorphosis from all angles. Kessler's face, his back, his ass, details of his hands and bare feet. At one point, he rolls over allowing us a pectoral view of the shift.

Landis' observation about the change of werewolf from monstrous person to afflicted sufferer rhymes with Kachuba, who similarly notes that

> as people lost their superstitious fears of demons and witches ... the werewolf became seen as a more sympathetic creature, one whose shape-shifting was more likely due to a curse put upon it than to any willful de-sire on the part of the human to change into a wolf

even, like Landis, naming *The Wolf Man* (after 1935's *Werewolf of London*) as an exemplar of this changed interpretation.

The person's experience of the metamorphosis as *physically* agonizing is central to eliciting our pity and/or revulsion. Naughton's writhing and agonized performance in *An American Werewolf in London* looks and sounds painful. I've mentioned earlier my hand stretching exercise? Here is its root—David Kessler's palm extending into the wolf-form's metacarpals. That image! Kessler looks on, his face still a white man's, in horror and pain, as though surgery is being performed on him without propofol. The toll of lycanthropic transformation had never seemed *skeletal* to me before—all dissolves and instant presto changos—but a matter of surfaces. This bone-deep sense was amplified by special sound effects creator Richard Lightman, who finds a perfect blend of moisture and clicking for the mobile bones reknitting under the motile flesh. Through it all, Kessler pleads for help and mercy, until his muzzle will no longer make the words, his teeth no longer doing anything but ribboning his English. The room goes dim, and I knew: the relation here wasn't Kessler *into* wolf, but wolf *of* Kessler.

And what a wolf! Admittedly, I favor bipedal lycanthropes, though should I reach my goal, I'd appreciate the ability to go quad for heightened speed (facilitated by the dogleg haunch). Baker's werewolf is a quadruped, but not just some big, nasty-looking wolf. The forelegs are elongated—the wolf slung forward and top-heavy. Its paws are articulated in such a way that they seem to remember being hands, the claws jutting and jutting.

There are times while writing when I lean back from the computer and my fingers go up to my mouth. Onychophagia. Nail-biting is another long-term project. When the nails are nubbed, the clipped, pale crescents binned or ground down, I work the skin around the cuticle. I'm thinking of a word as my teeth close in on a flap of flayed skin. Had I fangs, I could slice this frayed end right off. I'm thinking thinking of a word as I start to gnaw, to tug the skin away. There's an instant before it starts to sting, before what's revealed is too red and wet, that I might pull and pull, firmly like stripping the periosteum off a shank bone, and if I do this right, I could pull the skin off in one piece, revealing in a spiral of thin ribbon the meat underneath. Pulling the thin rind away in a slim, spiraling strip. I am thinking thinking thinking of a word when I realize what is happening. The hangnail tears off. I bite down hard on the whole distal phalanx. The crush of my blunt teeth's pressure shifts the pain from the torn skin to the whole thumb.

There is so much me in my stomach. More, perhaps, than what I've spat out. Person *in* person?

Two metamorphoses I'd like to add. One I've only seen in woodcut, the other I saw only recently as a clip in a YouTube video of "Best Werewolf Transformations" from Grumpy Andrew's Horror House.

The first: one could go into a wolf by pissing a ring around a wolfskin or your own clothes if you removed them, piled them up, and satisfied a few other environmental/sartorial conditions. The other, a scene from *Hemlock Grove*, a TV series, in which, following an optical demonstration, very much like the Huntsman, the werewolf eats his discarded human skin.

I have told you that I have practiced at something. Repeated it with an intention of preparation and inception. Becoming a werewolf. I do not practice reading my poems in this fashion. I read many of them as I work on them. This is generally part of a process of revision. I am readying them to be done with being written. But when I am asked after readings whether I practice my poems, this isn't what I figure most people to mean. I think they want to know whether I rehearse the poems for performance so that I may perform them well. And this kind of practice, I do not do.

Another question I am asked is whether I write poems the way I write them *because* of the skills I can bring to a performance or do I bring the skills because the poem requires them. There are things that I know I can do fairly well. Among these things number techniques that "work" in a context of live performance. They may not always work in every situation, just as certain compositional or rhetorical effects may not always work in every written situation, but I've paid attention to a lexicon of performance. Sometimes you pick things up. I do not mean to be coy: I want to push myself. I also want to experience pleasure. There are things I enjoy doing when I write, and some of these lead to familiar gestures to embody. Often, I work against them toward a generative estrangement. I am willing to make myself uncomfortable to serve a longer-term, elusive goal.

You may think, now, by talking about technique and not, say, content, I am avoiding discussing catharsis. Or that I have at last decided to stop talking about werewolves. No and no. For I am going to go into *catharsis*, rather, its absence through what has become an exercise in werewolf practice. A briar of control and change. Or release and relief.

For after queries of practice and process, another question I frequently receive is about catharsis. That is, are the poems cathartic?

No.

Writing them? No.

Reading them? No.

Not if the idea of catharsis includes release and relief in a relation, a logistic. One that could be described by way of a preposition? Writing and performing poems for me is not cathartic. Instead, these activities are a bit like tearing off a skin, then chewing it up.

Recall that a werewolf's injuries carry over between forms. This, I think, is a key way to understand why writing then performing the poems does not provide relief for me. Even if the poem provided an ersatz optical demonstration, whatever wound it seemed to take on would be there in the morning, under my fresh shirt, my untorn pants, my gargled maw. And even at the point of going through changes, it can be hard to discern or detangle pain and horror.

There are moments in my readings when I appear to get angry. I say "appear to get" to emphasize not the irony of perceiving my anger but the irony that it has suddenly seized me, as though a shield of dark clouds blocking the moon, gazing round and pale, has finally blown away. Like one of contemporary myths' most profitable lycanthropes, Bruce Banner, remarks in *The Avengers*: "That's my secret. . . . I'm always angry." The moon in my mind stays full. When in a reading I come

74

to a point in a poem where the irony, that which I have alloyed into the poem itself, gets to be a bit much; or, say, the poem's formal control is working too well, or, say, the poem is communicating a feel I feel unable to fully embody, I feel—how can I say it—a moment in which a part of me may double over. Something cramps, like a muscle I haven't prepared.

When I think about how best to read a poem aloud, I try to be *present* in the poem. To remember where I was—emotionally, psychologically —when I composed it, which is to put me closer to where I had been when what incited me to write it happened. Tracking it through all that's passed between the multiple points. But then, *as* I'm reading it, I must also be aware of who I am, the body I'm in, the conditions under which I've come to be present where I am in that body, and the bodies of the audience there with me as well. To be proprioceptive of a place I remember in a body from long ago, while I mean to know this one now.

"GET AWAY" is a difficult thing to say when your body is an invitation, even one you didn't make. If I say, "GET AWAY," who says it? After all, I knew the time, the pale moon's fullness, how dense the thicket.

There is a timbre I associate with these moments. It is one I know. One I remember. One I've learned over years of practice for nothing at all. For something that will probably never happen. I'm thinking thinking thinking thinking of a word and the skin is coming off me. My mouth a drawerful of cutlery.

When this happens at a reading, times are I can see the end of it, like a length of chain or expanse of fence. Other times, I only know that it can go into. On. Up. Down. Through. From. But never completely apart. I look down at my hands stretching toward the next page.

75

What I know about this is what the fourth grader, with his library book, tried to understand: the words alone won't do it. You need something else. Something to get into your skin. Something rubbed in. The words only take you to the edge of it. The words are a spell, a trigger, but not the thing itself, not the memory in your hands of what you've never been able to make them do. And that's why I don't find the poems cathartic. Not even when my voice finds the rest of me, and we're there as all we are, under that bright gaze. *What is cathartic about control?*

And I have practiced and practiced and practiced becoming a werewolf even longer than I've been writing poetry.

Now. Tell me: as the car is shuddering to a stop and the sounds of crickets and frogs creak around us in the falling darkness.

How good at it do you reckon I am?

"I'm not making metaphor."

RED/READ, READ/RED

PUTTING VIOLENCE DOWN IN POETRY

For Jason Yorrick, Roberto Ramos, Shihan Wong,
Sensei Wong, and to my Pops, Mom, and
Dallas Kearney for keeping me as safe as you could

During an Undergraduate
Writing Workshop I led, we came to a consensus about

content warnings for student submissions.

Suicidal ideation,

sexual violence,

and other forms of physical violence

would be noted in the header of each story or essay.

To reach that trio, students spitballed welters of extremis, abuse, and fight scenes. *Which ones would be* gratuitous?

Gratuitousness is a different metric than whether one scene might *be* violent. This was aesthetic judgment: does the scene serve the writing or is it just provocative?

At the same time as they were nuanced in their hypothetical scenarios, we never defined what *violence* itself is, even as we dismissed *psychological* and *emotional* harm from mandatory alert (though most students volunteered to report substance abuse). Critic J. David Slocum offers then complicates his definition of violence: "an action or behaviour that is harmful or injurious."

This seemed closest to our discussion and implied a tacit agreement that injury and hurt were principally *physical*, thus, a writer needn't warn us if incorporeality came to harm; only flesh was subject to triggerable damage.

Perhaps that's why, when prompting students to respond to weekly readings, I'd ask: "What *struck* you about the writing?" and nobody blinked.

Disclosure: sometimes it's hard for me to fret over written depictions of violence, particularly in literature's artifice; though I stay alert to who in a work suffers.

Yesterday, a mass shooting in Boulder, Colorado.

I better reckon such consideration's need the farther I get from figures of comparison—simile and metaphor, most especially.

Where I come from, comparing violences is a trap.

I sought to exhaust my Western poetics-trained drift toward figurative moves as principal evidence of skill.

I worked a taxonomic system in which I proposed tenors (the concept/image one means to describe) and vehicles (the concept/image bearing the symbolic weight) for bodies found in different settings, attitudes. I called it "An/Aesthetic."

TENOR	VEHICLE	SIGNIFICANT VARIATIONS
Prone/awry/faceup	High Cotton	Vegetal submissive: Sunup Vegetal symbiotic: Pickin Dat Vegetal dominant: Sundown
Prone/awry/facedown	Ka-Ka	Vegetal submissive: Scat Vegetal symbiotic: Poop Vegetal dominant: Dung

TENOR	VEHICLE	SIGNIFICANT VARIATIONS
Prone/plumb/ faceup	Level Playing Field	Vegetal submissive: Sand Trap Vegetal symbiotic: Fairway Vegetal dominant: Rough
Prone/plumb/ facedown	Rabbit	Vegetal submissive: Bugs Vegetal symbiotic: Brer Vegetal dominant: Watership

I created near 150 variations of about sixty vehicles. Placing and re-placing those corpses threatened to deaden me to their force.

Killing floors of disembodied metaphors.

As I write this, people in my community are talking about the trial for Derek Chauvin, the former member of the still active Minneapolis Police Department who, like countless cops before, murdered a Black man,

George Floyd.

People saying

Breonna Taylor,

a Black woman police also killed, among countless other murders of Black women. The community is thinking about Minneapolis's record-breaking $27 million settlement for Floyd's family. The $12 million Louisville paid Taylor's family drives questions of the value of Black life along gender lines, something asymmetric media attention to each murder exacerbates.

People are also talking about eight people, all but one, women, all but two, Asian and Asian American.

Soon Chung Park.

Hyun Jung Grant.

Suncha Kim.

Yong Ae Yue.

Delaina Ashley Yaun.

Paul Andre Michels.

Xiaojie Tan.

Daoyou Feng.

Now, Robert Aaron Long murdered all of *them*. Authorities are deciding what to call it besides the "Atlanta Spa Massacre."

Money called to represent life. Words debated to name violence's nature.

And there are other violences my community stays talking about. Disappeared Native women. Detention and deportation of Latinx people. Anti-Muslim attacks. Transphobic assaults. White nationalist terrorism. Neighborhood shootings. Systemic poverty.

Our mouths full of names, of blood.

What, here, is violence's nature named?

In "Bullet Points," Pulitzer Prize winner Jericho Brown writes:

> I promise if you hear
> Of me dead anywhere near
> A cop, then that cop killed me. He took
> Me from us and left my body, which is,
> No matter what we've been taught,
> Greater than the settlement
> A city can pay a mother to stop crying,

pointing at the inadequacy of money to represent a body subjected to violence. A speaker, here a person, a cop kills yet remains worth more than, say, twelve or even twenty-seven million dollars.

Still, Brown's powerful poem ends with the body:

> more beautiful than the new bullet
> Fished from the folds of my brain.

The speaker's body is *more* beautiful than the new bullet. This suggests the possibility of the bullet's beauty, that the bullet, drawn, shining, as a sleek fish might be from a glittering sea, could be beautiful.

If so, to whom but those who've taught us that we, too, can be lashed to money in a brutal metaphor?

Whose eye does the poet wish to catch by way of the bullet's *newness*, its bright clarity in the blood, the gray of the ravaged, deoxygenated human brain?

It occurred to me to make a taxonomy of poetic violence.

"Ambush": a violent disruption of language.

"Spatter": violence as ornament, embellishment.

"Gush": exaggerated, cartoonish violence.

"Spurt": sustained descriptions of violence.

"Slap": stylistically callous violence.

"Forensic": violence depicted with logistical rigor and a detached tone.

"Crop": writing where violence is only referenced, not described.

Yet, the more categories I created, the more I was manufacturing metaphors for metaphors. I thought of theorist Roland Barthes's assertion that myth gores out an existing language-object then occupies it, all the while feigning innocence of its parasitism.

I don't know whether taking a structuralist method of mythologization will make the violence more or less real.

I don't know which I prefer.

In *The Somnambulist*'s final stanza, Lara Mimosa Montes writes:

> eventually the moment cracks
> open as in life if this were life
> and to you I deliver the details
> like I would a bad dream

Prior, Montes reprints a facsimile of her uncle's criminal record, a "detail" of "life," a real *fact* in the reeling poem's waking dream of memory, trauma, myth.

But it isn't the poem's first fact:

     one is never safe
        so it is better to be ready
     to ride one's legends bareback

In Lucille Clifton's "jasper texas 1998," she writes as the head of James Byrd Jr. Three white nationalists murdered Byrd. They dragged him behind a pickup truck until, fishtailing, they swung him into a culvert, cutting off his head and arm. When Clifton writes,

> the arm as it pulled away
> pointed toward me, the hand opened once
> and was gone.

it is not "matter of fact"; this is a fictionalization. Neither is it precisely understatement. Is it "forensic"? "Pulled away" reminds us of the truck's inexorable horsepower as it peels off from the bloody culvert and wet dirt. As a pun, it doesn't take the shape of metaphor for me. Rather, its associative quality distributes force between the sense of *tearing* and *speeding*.

Left only with flesh, "pulling" seems to seek another material to affect. Something more viscous, like taffy, or something already begun breaking down. Here, I think, is violence: in the immediate, desperate sense that Clifton's word choice *gestures* toward the figurative.

Human bodies don't behave that way, they mustn't: they don't pull apart—, unless—

and we, the readers, execute the sequence of conditions necessary for the surreality of the poem to be drawn against a sense of understatement.

Like Clifton, I've written about James Byrd Jr. Introducing my poem "Big Thicket (Pastoral)," I lie down to demonstrate Byrd's position as the three white men dragged him.

This is dramatic reenactment, a trope of True Crime programs or courtroom dramas with flamboyant lawyers.

I note that the murderers pulled Byrd belly-down, his feet chained.

Forensically, this is an inversion of how I saw Hector dragged in a mythology book from my childhood. The illustrations were "realistic." I suppose this means they'd minimal stylization. A page I can't shake: the artist Rob McCaig's rendering of the minotaur. Thick pubic hair crept into a mat of brown strokes below its pale, taut abdomen and wiry thighs.

Homer, according to Richmond Lattimore, sets Achilles's desecration of Hector thusly:

> He spoke, and now thought of shameful treatment for glorious Hektor.
> In both of his feet at the back he made holes by the tendons
> in the space between ankle and heel, and drew thongs of ox-hide through
>   them,
> and fastened them to the chariot so as to let the head drag . . .

Knowledge of Hector's epithet—"of the shining helmet"—amplifies the brutalization; his helmetless head made filthy, run through the dust.

Perhaps you caught the scare quotes around "realistic." In deploying them, I am suggesting that I don't know whether the illustrated Hector was realistic: I've never seen anyone dragged behind a vehicle for *real*.

Were I in Jasper on June 7, 1998, I still might not have seen the dragging: it was dark. As the truck pulled away, what besides taillights would've lit Huff Creek Road? The moon? Streetlamps?

Yet when we call a description of violence we've never witnessed "realistic" what do we mean?

I am reminded of film critic Stephen Prince, who, discussing Mel Gibson's 2004 *The Passion of the Christ*, wrote:

> The viewers measured Gibson's movie against other Hollywood depictions of Jesus' torture and crucifixion. The film's graphic violence was judged to be "realistic" in comparison with the pre-existing cinematic tradition of sanitized and oblique depictions of crucifixion.

Applying this to poetry, what genres create a comparative tradition of violence? Middle Passage poetry. Slavery poetry. Lynching poetry. How do their constitutive poems leave them with flickering red, pitch darkness, or blanching, shadow-throwing light?

The murderers didn't necessarily *accuse* James Byrd Jr. of anything. Thus, Clifton's and my poems are not *lynching poems*. Though, maybe, adjacent.

I'm talking genre because I've something unsavory for taxonomies, and, as Prince argues, genre offers contexts in which we reckon representations of violence. Film theorists, including John Cawelti, Judith Hess Wright, and Thomas Schatz concur.

We might expect *The Iliad*, a war epic, to depict carnage. Or anti-war poetry, say, Wilfred Owen's "Dulce et Decorum Est," to detail brutality.

> Gas! GAS! Quick, boys!—An ecstasy of fumbling
> Fitting the clumsy helmets just in time,
> But someone still was yelling out and stumbling
> And flound'ring like a man in fire or lime.—
> Dim through the misty panes and thick green light,
> As under a green sea, I saw him drowning.

Owen's *ecstasy* signals transcendence, mocking war as "glory" with a secondary definition: "religious frenzy." Veneration struck from this muddle of clumsy, stumbling, floundering death, awash in sick green.

In "Welter," a poem about the genocidal campaign against Rohingya Muslims, I echo Owen.

> Sic on it, cameras: queasy-green lush rush canopy—tilt down: thick bamboo cover twine-bound—tilt down: welter, dirt's got rags to gag up, hijab stuck in dun incisors—zoom in and rack . . .

Owen's poem's an eyewitness account. Mine is worked up from photographs and imagination. A secondhand spurt.

The camera is violence's frequent mediator. Consider the Motion Picture Producers and Distributors of America's 1927 admonishment that filmmakers take "special care" in their treatment of subjects subject to potential "vulgarity" and "suggestiveness." The MPPDA came up with twenty-five "Be Carefuls." Here are fourteen.

3. Arson;
4. The use of firearms;
5. Theft, robbery, safe-cracking, and dynamiting of trains, mines, buildings, et cetera . . .;
6. Brutality and possible gruesomeness;
7. Technique of committing murder by whatever method;
10. Actual hangings or electrocutions as legal punishment for crime;
11. Sympathy for criminals;
14. Apparent cruelty to children and animals;
15. Branding of people or animals;
16. The sale of women, or of a woman selling her virtue;
17. Rape or attempted rape;
22. Surgical operations;
23. The use of drugs;
24. Titles or scenes having to do with law enforcement or law-enforcing officers;

It may be off-color noting how much of my traditions' content—Black poets' work—would be on these editors' killing floor. Poetry about the *peculiar institution* (*i.e.*, slavery) could tick off fourteen, easy.

Still, tradition isn't genre. And Black poetry hasn't had the taxonomical work-overs of fiction.

Let's try. Lynching poetry. Slavery poetry. Middle Passage poetry etc.

A lynching poem might require as its inciting event an accusation followed by an execution, *without* legal trial. Poems of Christ's torture and crucifixion don't fit. Do stanzas of his punishment at the hands of the state constitute a genre?

Could a tradition begin here?

And they stripped him, and put on him a scarlet robe.

And when they had platted a crown of thorns, they put it upon his head, and a reed in his right hand: and they bowed the knee before him, and mocked him, saying, Hail, King of the Jews!

And they spit upon him, and took the reed, and smote him on the head.

. . . they crucified him . . . (Matthew 27:28–30, 35)

Here?

And they smote him on the head with a reed, and did spit upon him, and bowing their knees worshipped him.

. . . they crucified him. (Mark 15:19, 25)

Here?

Then Pilate therefore took Jesus, and scourged him.

And the soldiers platted a crown of thorns, and put it on his head, and they put on him a purple robe,

And said, Hail, King of the Jews! and they smote him with their hands.

... they crucified him ... (John 19:1–3, 18)

And are these oblique?

This?

> But they cried out, saying:
> Crucify him!—
> Crucify him!—
> Crucify him!—
> His blood be on our heads,
> And they beat my loving Jesus,
> They spit on my precious Jesus;
> They dressed him up in a purple robe,
> They put a crown of thorns upon his head,
> And they pressed it down—
> Oh, they pressed it down—
> And they mocked my sweet King Jesus.
>
> JAMES WELDON JOHNSON, from "The Crucifixion"

Johnson uses cries to "Crucify him" diegetically. The crowd chants, demanding Christ's execution. This repetition both amplifies and distills the Sanhedrin's exchange with Pilate. Refrain works differently at: "And they pressed it down— / Oh, they pressed it down." Repetition *and* revision, a familiar tool in Black sonic art. Aesthetics are significant here, but this nod to sermonizing's orality also *prolongs* the wounding of Christ's brow. A slow-motion or sustained shot.

Diegesis, amplification, and rep&rev saturate this stanza:

> On Calvary, on Calvary,
> They crucified my Jesus.

95

They nailed him to the cruel tree,
And the hammer!
The hammer!
The hammer!
Rang through Jerusalem's streets.
The hammer!
The hammer!
The hammer!
Rang through Jerusalem's streets.

Johnson crops the violence off-page, such that we perceive the hammer as a *metonym* of Christ's torment.

Diegesis. As Greek as *The Iliad*, its etymology leads to "narrative." *Diegetic*—however, runs through English (*-etic*) to become, if not a French word, a Gallic concept, suggesting, "In the writer's own voice." As *narrative* is a component in the machine of story, *diegetic* describes *sound* in the context of a story or sound in a film that the characters hear. Non-diegetic sound—say, a film's score—isn't audible to the characters in the film, but to us.

HAMMER! HAMMER! HAMMER! HAMMER! HAMMER!

Diegetic sound passes through the written world into ours. Blood soaks through paper.

Is onomatopoeia, I wonder, ever non-diegetic?

KRAK! KRAK! KRAK! goes my poem about James Byrd Jr., "Big Thicket (Pastoral)."

In 2004, when I shared the first draft in a workshop at Callaloo, my classmate Jericho Brown said KRAK! conjured the sound of sticks breaking, tromped by heavy boots in the darkness of woods.

KRAK! appears suddenly, an ambush suggesting so many violences in the poem's diegetic space.

"A KRAK is a stick broke," "KRAK is a buckshot," "a KRAK is fists boots bone."

"HuffKRAK! HuffKRAK!"—KRAK is Huff Creek Road, itself, accessory to murderers killing Byrd Jr.

KRAK, twenty-two times in the poem.

HAMMER! HAMMER! HAMMER!

KRAK! KRAK! KRAK!

Éden, Éden, Éden, by French novelist Pierre Guyotat, is one of the most violent things I've read.

Etymologically, its title reads *Delightful Place, Delightful Place, Delightful Place*.

Éden, Éden, Éden fever-dreams the French-Algerian War in a single, spurting sentence of pornography and barbarity. It's easy to assume I use those words in prudish judgment, but that's some of what Guyotat's on about. It begins:

> / Soldiers, helmets cocked down, legs spread, trampling, muscles drawn back, over new-born babes swaddled in scarlet, violet shawls: babies falling from arms of women huddled on floors of G.M.C. trucks; driver's free hand pushing back goat thrown forward into cab . . . stone walls oozing spattered with brains, orchards blooming, palmtrees, swollen in fire, exploding: flowers, pollen, buds, grasses, paper, rags spotted with milk, with shit, with blood . . .

Rather, it begins: "Now we are no longer slaves."

Who's no longer a slave? To whom? Or what?

This work of sexual(ized) violence and aesthetic transgression, what Roland Barthes prefaces as "language and lust . . . in a reciprocal metonymy," continues a tradition of white artists pursuing innovation through their representations of Black and Brown bodies as a subject and site.

A *delightful place* for some fuckery.

Repetition—lexical (say, *Éden, Éden, Éden*), cultural (Black and Brown bodies as sites for white aesthetic transgression), or historical (Black and Brown bodies as sites for white transgression) can be percussive or numbing on the page. Striking sharply then, perhaps, droning—no longer felt or perceived as articulated. The repetition saturates until there is no longer paper, only blood, thus the page is no longer *wet* but, itself, a liquid, no longer a container of *information*—blood as presence—over there, sealed in the *b*, *l*, *o*'s, *d*—now, the blood is everywhere, and nowhere, especially not on this piece of paper.

Repetition as anaphora is, for some, a saturation become stylistically oversaturated. The predictability of its repetition, I guess, hits some ears as cosplaying at poetic eloquence, incantation as a conspicuous ceremonial quality dulled with overuse.

Anaphora is the banal language of jurisprudence, policies, and bureaucracies that abstract human selfhood in the name of power, commerce, and violent control.

Anaphora is a device that may anesthetize before wounding.

Is that what irks some when they encounter it? Not that it diminishes chant but, like it, insists transparently on affecting us, language as flesh, undeterred by the rational mind?

Whereas it could take as long as 16 seconds between the trigger pulled in Las Vegas and the Hellfire missile landing in Mazar-e-Sharif, after which they will ask *Did we hit a child? No. A dog.* they will answer themselves;

. . . .

Whereas the lover made my heat rise, rise so that if heat sensors were trained on me, they could read my THERMAL SHADOW through the roof and through the wardrobe;

. . . .

Whereas I cannot control my own heat and it can take as long as 16 seconds between the trigger, the Hellfire missile, and *A dog* . . .

Whereas *A dog*, they will say: Now, therefore,

Let it matter what we call a thing.

Solmaz Sharif's *Look* wields anaphora—"whereas . . . whereas . . . whereas . . ."—not to contain violence and sex (the missile, the speaker's heat, thermal shadow, an imploding aubade to be exploded by drone strike, all hot and bothering, dogging speaker and reader); rather *doing* violence and sex via law's performative language, which reproduces its power through droning, lexical slow-fucking, authorizing the flesh/blood fucking up of others on its behalf. Sharif's speaker's lover a trigger hovering over her waiting for the next *whereas* which becomes *let* (allow, rent, bleed) as we look.

Layli Long Soldier writes:

Whereas precedes and invites.

What is it to precede without invitation—to be one for whom "whereas" abets necropolitical power? To be the white man in *WHEREAS*:

Whereas his wrist loose at the bottleneck he comes across as candid "Well, *at least* there was an Apology, that's all I can say" he offers to the circle each of them scholarly;

. . . .

Whereas I could've but didn't broach the subject of "genocide" the absence of this term from the Apology and its rephrasing as "conflict" for example;

He elides that he *can* wield "whereas," not from "great imagination or a work of fiction," but authority, like the "whereas" Long Soldier wrests from President Obama's non-apology for *not-genocide*.

Genocide Long Soldier broaches throughout *WHEREAS* the collection, "Whereas Statements" the poem, and "38," presencing thirty-eight Dakota men, hanged in "the largest 'legal' mass execution in US history."

Legal. So not a lynching, but a state-authorized flesh/blood fucking up of Dakota men.

"38," which does not seek to be "a 'creative piece,'" works the language of what's not creative (murder, famine) such that:

One should read "The Dakota people starved" as a straightforward and plainly stated fact.

The facts, she leaves:

bones.

Violence as entertainment is a pop-cultural sure shot. I say I write about violence because I am compelled by its intersection with spectacle. The *extra*legal executions of Black people turned postcard material, news cycle bonanza, the head on a stake by Liberty's gated community.

The fact of it, like the fact of programmatic Native American genocide, fills my mind, my pages. I type the word *blood*. Another fact. There is blood. Type it again. My exhausted imagination a welter of red, red, red.

What such need to keep blood fresh?

In "A Little Black," Brendan Constantine discloses:

> The children of Juarez have run out
> of red crayons. There's so much blood
>
> in their eyes; the bodies of mules
> dumped in their schools, hands & heads
>
> by the road, blood in pools, blood
> in stories of blood. Before I know it,
>
> I'm planning my own crime, the worst
> a poet can commit: to steal suffering . . .

I share Constantine's cold dread that poetry can be vampiric via the violent transmutation of the literal into the figurative. Imagine him at "Letter I," writing the stunning:

"A sword is an oar to paddle through men."

Imagine him pulling away, horrified by such beautiful craft.

On Rachel Zucker's *Commonplace*, Robin Coste Lewis remarks:

> Beauty is a dark, heinous, sublime, awe-inspiring thing . . . Black, strong, iron, unapologetic.

Lewis's *dark* and *black* are and aren't racial, as historic uses of darkness and blackness are racial and not. She contrasts "beauty" with "prettiness," one letter shy of *pettiness*. The sublime is the precinct of awe, which is a kind of fear. Contact with the divine that, Anne Carson reminds us on *Bookworm*, pulverizes us.

At least that's how it is in the Greek myths.

Greek myths, we been taught, are worthy of rapt consideration, passing like new bullets through genres, media, frequently with aspirational reverence.

Beauty by association.

Yeats's "Leda and the Swan," I recall from high school, has Zeus's raping Leda as a sonnet, with a "broken" eleventh line.

We are to understand this as "mastery," disciplined balance of passion (the vividness of Yeats's poetics) and distance (the material: myth; rape reduced to trope). I mean to contrast this with his divine rapist's control, whose "indifferent beak" dispatches the volta.

We are to reckon what Leda cannot, vague as the Master has her, in his spattered glory of rush/lies, dead/up, power/drop.

A sonnet is, perhaps, apt for threats: voltas inexorably upset what we've been made to know, unsettling an established order.

The first four lines of Carl Phillips's "Ransom" are menacing—there's an activity that whips us beyond suspended ominousness.

> How he was carried in a ramshackle cart alongside the sea.
> How he lay on his side, on a bed of straw—
> mules pulling the cart; the straw
> for the blood . . .

Even the cart seems beaten. Later, we'll learn the mules, like the abducted, are broken. The title looms in its tacit threat of what comes should the ransom price remain unmet.

Phillips has us eye the youth (why is it a youth in my mind, the eros of his body against littoral profile?); what violence has been done; it's unclear whether the straw lies blood-sopped or splayed dry for blood soon come.

In medias res is penetration.

And the blood? "Not as in power but the echo of it, and the echo fading . . ." Phillips's speaker interrupts the traffic between blood and power, the former an attenuation of the latter. I'm never sure I trust the narrator, sitting, it seems to me, at the right hand of the man with the whip.

KRAK!

Whip doesn't only mean slavery—even set against broken mules. And still, when a whip appears in a Black person's art, how many press, generically, the cowhide into peculiar service?

And *where* whip signifies enslavement in a Black poet's poem, it may still be entangled with otherwise.

In "Black Memorabilia," CM Burroughs works the precarious frisson of pain and sensuality she's suffered to master.

> . . . My beloved feature of the Black man is his edge, the tender shape of
> Otherness, careful valley of chain. When he fucks me, isn't he uprising?
> Stealing back his mother/sister/woman bound by light? I let the tension
> move through me. Try not to scream. Try to bear the whip of umbilical
> cords, breasts and bone. To be entered. To be exited . . .

Like artist FKA Twigs, Burroughs brings bodies to abstraction (*he*: threshold, *she*: bondage system). Then, Burroughs thrusts them back into flesh (that which can enter/be entered, can steal/be stolen) before reverting to invert their abstractions. *She* turns border to cross; *he* may come to contain her via conception's umbilical whip, lashing her to— rather than severing her from—family. Their dark, sublime sex violent enough she must steel against screaming.

Still, some violence in "Black Memorabilia" lies waiting past the cane-brake tryst. "Isn't he uprising?" Stealing back? "There is danger in how we see one another," Burroughs writes. Danger. Let's call it in one of its names.

Lynching.

A lynching is a performance. An act of site-specific theater. I'm not making metaphor.

Lynchings have played before crowds large and small. And when the troupe hears crickets and not whoops of approval, the show tends to go on.

Those lynched are quadruple threats: they are the stars, the props, snack bar, and souvenirs. They are naturals—the supporting cast *yes ands* them into ovation. I'm not making metaphor.

Amaud Jamaul Johnson's "Burlesque" centers around a lynched man. Johnson's indispensable collections grapple with violence and entertainment in ways I do not, with cold irony in metaphor. It becomes possible to imagine the deep figures of his restaging as reciprocal, not substitutions.

> Watch the fire undress him,
> how flame fingers each button,
> rolls back his collar, unzips him
> without sweet talk or mystery.
>
> See how the skin begins to gather
> at his ankles, how it slips into

the embers, how it shimmers
beneath him, unshapen, iridescent,

. . . .

how his whole body becomes song . . .

"i set this place ablaze," ends Aurielle Marie's "gxrl gospel i: all the women were white, all of the Black folk, men & so we were brave"; the title itself a documentary of violence, a disappearing in an intersection, the danger in how many don't see Black womxn in danger.

trans

> Forming our many deaths into inheritance—defying
> the cleavers and tar, the barbed wire, the boiling oil, the
> torch fire, the porch bombs, the addled calls, severed
> brake lines or draggings behind wagons, drowned or
> thrown down the well . . .

Marie's litany of the many deaths, its many names, its number made more potent for the deaths and dangers it doesn't contain—what name will you say, reader? Made more potent for Marie's specificity, murder scenes cropped to concentrated iconographies.

No substitutions here either—death isn't *transformed* into a cash settlement through Marie's "inheritance." Death stay death. What strikes me is that, despite the accumulated deaths, for the Black womxn to inherit them is to first know *life* against dangers named, unnamed, and nameless.

That, then, is what intensifies the violence Marie unshackles in the poem's title. That our erasure of Black womxn disinherits them of death, thus: life.

"Violence," Dawn Lundy Martin asserts, "like other traumas, fragments the self and removes the ground from below us."

The poet and critic is introducing *Is God Is*, Aleshea Harris's ferocious play in which twin sisters, each burned, strike out for retribution on their father, who set their mother ablaze when they were toddlers.

Reading the play, I reel under Harris's elemental, dirty dirty treatment of dialogue:

> We ain't animals. We on a mission. From God.
>
> . . . .
>
> I mean we floatin
> We land from time to time and get stepped on but thas it.
>
> . . . .
>
> ## Make him dead real dead
> And bring me back some treasures from it.

But when I encounter the stage directions, my sense splits. I am reading violence to be embodied—the stylistic change between Harris's dialogue and paratextual instructions:

> *Sound of rock hitting flesh and ANAIA retching.*

and

> *She hits him again and again until he gurgles, twitches, and is still.*

Ionesco's (playfully?) callous aspiration toward destruction of human forms finds discordant chime in Jennif(f)er Tamayo's theatrical, unsettling gusto.

In "ONCE I DANCED WITH A MAN YOU LOOKED LIKE AND I HAD RIPPED THE FACE FROM OFF YOUR BODY," a strafed critique of gendered body-shaming leans carnal with B flicks' exuberant ultraviolence:

> You need to make room . . . Cram them in, she thought. Cram them in. Cut their limbs off. Put their bodies through a strainer. Liquefy the people and animal bodies. You dream of hot entrails.

Here, in "IF YOU, THE FATHER, IS THE DEATH OF ALL THINGS, YOU LACK AT ME & FEEL NARCISSUS," Tamayo ruptures perseverating anaphora with pop spurts.

> So hungry I swallow my oh my! So hungry I swallow my oh nah-nah what's my name? So hungry I swallow my whole face. So hungry I'll swallow your hole face.

The speaker's mouth devours selfhoods as punctuation reels from interjection to interrogation to declaration, audaciously cannibalized and cannibalizing. Whole (complete) becomes hole (*incomplete*) face; a bloody mine where the speaker digs for what's theirs (*my* oh my, my name, my face).

Tamayo's is a gush of carnivalesque violence; not as catharsis, but in its ferocious abandonment of constraint and/with flesh.

Abandoning constraint *and* flesh.

Abandoning constraint *with* flesh.

The first ruptures limit—one of discipline and one of materiality.

The second refuses to recognize a material limit to preserve its integrity. I mean to mean that to abandon constraint *with* flesh is to visit radical transformation upon it. Destruction, perhaps, or like Ionesco muttering in the darkened wings, a metaphor willed real.

In Gwendolyn Brooks's genius work "The Last Quatrain of the Ballad of Emmett Till," she works with *with*:

AFTER THE MURDER,

AFTER THE BURIAL

Emmett's mother is a pretty-faced thing;
    the tint of pulled taffy.
She sits in a red room,
    drinking black coffee.
She kisses her killed boy.

How Mamie's pretty face (flesh), like pulled taffy, is sweet, then bitter, knelling with Till's mutilated face. A face reflected in dark liquid, the coffee Mamie, whose lips Emmett's favor, sips, as if to kiss the face that is their shared pretty face, pulled now, one from the other, through murder's red room. How *taffy* and *coffee* come with slant chime in sound and sense. What can be consumed. Brooks's violence of figurativeness points toward the white men who abandoned constraint with Emmett's flesh; points toward, doesn't pull away.

After the murder, before the burial, turning and turning goes Marilyn Nelson's *A Wreath for Emmett Till*, a virtuoso heroic crown of sonnets. Central to the poem is *witness*; yet, the strophe beginning "Like the full moon, which smiled calmly on his death" is a series of eight similes. What does simile have us see?

> Like wildflowers growing beside the path
> a boy was dragged along, blood spattering
> their white petals as he, abandoning
> all hope, gasped his agonizing last breath.
>
> . . . .
>
> Like a gouged eye, watching boots kick a face.

I distrust simile; it often abets false equivalency's ontological violence. Nelson wields this imprecision to undermine simile's imperative to look away by drawing vehicles (objects of comparison) from the murder scene while suspending tenors (subjects of comparison). Thus, *all we see* is the violence, even as the comparator ("like") signals we should find something else to regard.

Similarly, Nelson's allusion to the third canto of Dante's *Inferno*'s ("abandoning / all hope") narrates/amplifies Till's diegetic gasp. Allusion's subtlety (versus reference's conspicuousness) allows us to stay in the poem, a poem whose form (cruelly) demands recursion and volta despite the reality that Till won't breathe again and *that* won't change.

In a course I teach where students create poetic forms, we discussed *chime*. Segueing into reckoning politics reconstructed through prosodies and poetics, a student posted:

Chime and containment.

We came to reckon chime—rhyme, say—segments and delimits, though a flexible scheme might not assert a *discernible* pattern of regulation.

The student, working through philosophers György Lukács and Frantz Fanon in another course, was responding to Glyn Maxwell, who, in *On Poetry*, described reading a densely patterned rhyme scheme as being

herded into a shrinking space where only these sounds can be uttered.

My student sought a liberatory poetics. One that won't reproduce or reenact strategies of colonial violence. One laying bare its political origins.

Consider: what are Spanish *castas* but means of tracking chime, identifying what is perfect, slant, rising, falling against the scheme's "A"—a masculine Spaniard?

Natasha Trethewey takes this up throughout her collection *Thrall*. Here, from the first strophe of "The Americans":

To strip from the flesh
　　the specious skin; to weigh
　　　　in the brainpan

                    seeds of white
              pepper; to find in the body
                    its own diminishment—

Brutality, rebranded as enlightened surgical inquiry, Trethewey re-
minds us, spurred by an urge to

                    still know white from not.

In the genre-agnostic, lyric *scenery*, José Felipe Alvergue reckons with Spanish *casta* categories, the carceral state, and nationalist rallies—each a context of systemic violence within and against which, fearfully, he holds his child. In the face of

looking

upon the catastrophic evidence

of order

Alvergue rejects optimism and searches for meaninglessness. Ever interrogating, his position in networks of domination and repression, Alvergue takes wide views of public history before retreating to the domestic private. While one can identify violence in individual lines and phrases, Alvergue, like Massin and Harris, uses visual composition to enact irruptive conflict: found text collides into his own at sharp angles. Archival images shatter his present.

Careful. In *scenery*, a simmering anger "has frothed among pages of study."

Froth is a substance near light as air. Froth foments, like riots.

We are left floating and piecemeal in the wake of violence.

Dawn Lundy Martin says, again, introducing a play in which God is a person who can burn like any sinner.

material apparatus of a theatrical stage

violent encounter between two or more persons

in front of, before (as in evident)

In introducing *scenery*, José Felipe Alvergue says:

Theorizing nihilism . . . in
the apocalypse of emotion

Alvergue and I attended grad school together. He was constructively skeptical about my thesis, an opera in which I created a counterfeit language, translation of which, contested by dramatic action and scenic design that obscured projected supertitles, would stand in for cultural appropriation. Specifically, white appropriation of Black cultural production, a procedure I understood as extractive, exploitative, and, ultimately, eradicating.

I've just written this litany for the first time, and I feel a way about how it matches steps in the choreography of ecological plunder. I feel a way, understand, about how such a chime revives for some, incepts for others a sense that Black culture is *like* a natural resource. This, in an ontological gaffle, erases the fact of that culture as *already cultivated*. As in worked. As in developed. As in something other than scenery against which whiteness can hack its jackleg-mastery skit-work.

It occurs to me that Alvergue's "apocalypse of emotion" might be the definition of opera I've needed.

Apocalypse—a word frequently used these days to denote a cataclysmic ending, but etymologically means to uncover, to reveal.

Thus, the transparent liberatory poetics my student seeks? Apocalyptic in its origins.

The curtain rises, breaking open a world.

I've written several opera libretti, now, and most end in annihilation. By this, I mean to mean that not just a lead character dies but much of the staged world, too—death revealing itself, sudden and total.

Mordake, having swallowed all but his sister Brigit's face, sets to finish the job.

A hurricane wipes out *Crescent City*'s denizens, Marie Laveau floating off (cataclysm!).

Sucktion's Irona disappears with her fritzing vacuum cleaner into a cloud of steam and ozone.

Nanzee oversees *Benbannik*'s ruinous bloodbath.

Jiggaboobonic becomes a human bomb at a police substation.

Sweet Land closes with a wasteland of ghosts.

Dead Horses spends its run time dying, the swarming flies a sundial's shade.

I wonder about my disinterest in the idea of these characters existing after the curtain falls. This isn't quite right; the countdown begins when the curtain *rises*.

Opera interests me because it announces its artifice. As a *work*, the weight of that artifice, the weight of its apocalypse is distributed among several artists.

Yet, when I write a poem, is it I imagine *I* should literally explode or collapse like my language; my head should become detached from my body, my arms and legs flying to pieces, etc.?

And if one flew to pieces, would this only mean disintegration?

I remember David Dabydeen's *Turner*, a long poem, in part, an ekphrasis of J. M. W. Turner's *The Slave Ship (Slavers Throwing overboard the Dead and Dying—Typhon coming on*, 1840). *Turner* proposes that the limbs in the painting's foreground draw together, becoming amalgamations of consciousness.

The Slave Ship is not "realistic" but *detailed*. A lurid nightmare. Shackled wrists and ankles break the surface as grotesque fish surge out the red welter.

> The women are less familiar
> But I name them Adra, Zentu, Danjera,
> The names of my mother and my father's wives.
>
> . . . .
>
> The sea prepares
> Their festive masks, salt crystals like a myriad
> Of sequins hemmed into their flesh . . .
>
> . . . .
>
> The sea decorates, violates.
> Limbs break off, crabs roost between their breasts
> Feeding. The sea strips them clean. I am ashamed
> To look upon the nakedness of my mothers.

Dabydeen re-members this horror and the lives preceding it through the collaged subjectivities of his new speaker(s). That the beings are

shattered and collected parallels trauma that persists in a violated col-
lective (un)consciousness; a violation normatively visited here upon
mothers, wives. Does a reductive trope swan in? Does *Turner* slip that
yoke?

Middle Passage poems often address the trade's mutilating force with formal re-enactment. Collage, erasure, versioning, detournement, and conjure, each involve intentional disruption, often of the self.

Robert Hayden and M. NourbeSe Philip cleave testimonies. Hayden's "Middle Passage" is a masterpiece, which Kwame Dawes notes

> is made up of a pastiche of the many white voices engaged in the slave trade.

I don't read this as a sop to the modern Westerner's fragmented psyche; rather a roundup of suspects (plus: "Be Carefuls" 3, 6, 7, and 17):

> "That when the Bo's'n piped all hands, the flames
> spreading from starboard already were beyond
> control, the negroes howling and their chains
> entangled with the flames:
>
> "That the burning blacks could not be reached,
> that the Crew abandoned ship,
> leaving their shrieking negresses behind,
> that the Captain perished drunken with the wenches:
>
> "Further Deponent sayeth not."

A genius work of haunting, Philip's *Zong!* recovers lives from "brutal abstraction" (see: Stephanie Smallwood). A legal document for the slaver *Zong*, whose crew falsified negligent deaths of more than one hundred captives as an insurance loss, becomes a doorway through which voices return. The guttering, drowning

w w w   w a wa

in my mouth creates a somatic halting, matching the gapped typesetting.

Public Enemy's "Can't Truss It" interrogates the Middle Passage and its wake.

Chuck D, lyrical terrorist, busts:

> Now the story that I'm kickin' is gory . . .

Punning on Gorée Island, home to a slave fortress off Senegal, and *gory* as in gruesome, Chuck makes a statement about genre—a story of the transatlantic slave trade will be gory. Anything less would be to sugarcoat it, reproducing slavery apologists' reports on the system's brutality.

> Rollin' in my own leftover
> When I roll over, I roll over in somebody else's
>
> . . . .
>
> Three months pass, they brand a label on my ass

The first describes the shit sloshing in slavers' holds so cramped that captives—sick with the bloody flux and fear—reeled in each other's excrement. Branded bodies ("Be Careful" #15) here are literal brands *and* a reference to brand names on jeans—signifying ownership.

Harryette Mullen's "[Kills bugs dead]" puns the Middle Passage from a contemptuous contemporary whose dream (the American one, perhaps) is haunted by the deadly cruise's legacy of dehumanization.

> Their noise infects the dream. . . . they foul the food, walk on our bodies
> as we sleep over oceans of pirate flags.

Know hungry vermin, too, occupied the leftovers of those left.

There is more to say.

But I don't know what I want you to know anymore.

An apocalypse of—

I can't even say what I thought to make plain.

Except perhaps once again

when folx in my community are talking about the trial for Derek Chauvin, the former member of the still active Minneapolis Police Department who, like countless cops before, murdered a Black man,

George Floyd.

Folx are saying

Breonna Taylor,

a Black woman police also killed, among countless other murders of Black women. We are thinking about Minneapolis's record-breaking $27 million settlement for Floyd's family. The $12 million Louisville paid Taylor's family is driving questions of the value of Black life along gender lines, exacerbated by asymmetric media attention to both murders.

My community is also talking about eight people, all but one, women, all but two, Asian and Asian American.

Soon Chung Park.

Hyun Jung Grant.

Suncha Kim.

Yong Ae Yue.

Delaina Ashley Yaun.

Paul Andre Michels.

Xiaojie Tan.

Daoyou Feng.

Robert Aaron Long murdered all of them. Authorities are deciding what to call it besides the "Atlanta Spa Massacre."

Money called to represent life. Words debated to name violence's nature.

And there are other violences my community stays talking about. Disappeared Native women. Detention and deportation of Latinx people. Anti-Muslim attacks. Transphobic assaults. White nationalist terrorism. Neighborhood shootings. Systemic poverty. Our mouths full of names and—

"I'm not making metaphor.
I'm not making metaphor.
I'm not making metaphor.
I'm not making metaphor."

RED/READ, READ/RED

VERSION

A Collaboration with Val-Inc

During an Undergraduate Writing Workshop course,
the class came to a consensus content warnings
spitballed a montage of abuse and fight scenes.
"Be Carefuls."

montage of abuse and fight scenes.

violence itself   *gratuitous?*

"Be Carefuls." admonishment that filmmakers take "special care"
Suicidal Ideation, sexual violence.
spitballed a   and other forms of physical violence
should be noted
montage of abuse and fight scenes.
gratuitous? "Be Carefuls."

what *struck* you about the writing?

the Motion Picture Producers and   the class came to   3. Arson;
Distributors of America's 1927 *struck*   the class came to
                                              the class came to   4. The use of firearms;
5. Theft, robbery, safe-cracking and dynamiting of trains, mines, buildings, et cetera
6. Brutality and possible gruesomeness; 7. Technique of committing murder
"Be Carefuls."   by whatever method; ...
10. Actual hangings or electrocutions as legal punishment for crime;
14. Apparent cruelty to children and animals; 11. Sympathy for criminals; ...
15. Branding of people or animals;   "Be Carefuls."
16. The sale of women, or of a woman selling her virtue;
"Be Carefuls.' 17. Rape or attempted rape; ...
22. Surgical operations;
23. The use of drugs;
24.Titles or scenes having to do with law enforcement or law-enforcing officers;

a taxonomy of
violence.violence.
violence.

AAAAA

"Ambush": a violent disruption of image or language.

one is never safe **IIIII**

I

"Spatter": violence as ornament, embellishment.

FFFFF!!!!!!

"Gush": exaggerated, cartoonish violence.

don't **OOOOO** know

"Spurt": sustained descriptions of violence.

HH HH w**HH**hich

"Slap": stylistically callous violence.

N N NN NN

"Forensic": violence depicted with logistical rigor.

OOOO!O!!!!!!

"Crop": writing where violence is only referenced,
one is never safe
not described.

the more categories I created, the more I saw myself
manufacturing metaphors for metaphors.

I don't know which I prefer.

The MPPDA Guyotat Constantine Tamayo Harris Long Soldier
Burroughs Sharif Chuck D Hayden Trethewey Brown

—amplifies the brutalization. here

Consider the Motion Picture Producers and
Distributors of America's 1927 admonishment that filmmakers
take "special care" in their treatment of subjects subject to potential
"vulgarity" and "suggestiveness." The MPPDA came up with 25 "Be
Carefuls." Here are 14.

3. Arson; |palm-trees, swollen in fire, exploding:

4. The use of firearms; KRAK! KRAK! KRAK! KRAK!
Blood soaks through paper.

5. Theft, robbery, I'm planning my own crime, the worst
safe-cracking, and dynamiting a poet can commit: to steal suffering...
of trains, mines, buildings, et cetera...

6. Brutality and possible gruesomeness; Cram them in. Cut their limbs off.
Put their bodies through a strainer.

7. Technique of committing murder Blood soaks through paper.
by whatever method; ... She hits him again and again until
he gurgles, twitches, and is still.

10. Actual hangings or electrocutions 38 Dakota men, hanged in
as legal punishment for crime; "the largest 'legal'
mass execution in US history."

11. Sympathy for criminals; ... ... My beloved feature of the Black man is
his edge, the tender shape of Otherness,

14. Apparent cruelty to children and animals; after which they will ask
Did we hit a child? No. A dog.
they will answer themselves...

...and three months past
15. Branding of people or animals; they brand a label on my ass

16. The sale Blood soaks th
of women, or of a woman "That Crew and Captain lusted with the comeliest
selling her virtue; rough paper of the savage girls kept naked in the cabins;
17. Rape or attempted rape; ... and they cast lots and fought to lie with her

22. Surgical operations; To strip from the flesh
23. The use of drugs; the specious skin; to weigh
in the brainpan

24.Titles or scenes having to do with law I promise if you hear
enforcement or law-enforcing officers; Of me dead anywhere near
A cop, then that cop killed me.

137

It may be off-color noting how much of my traditions' content—Black poets' work — would be on these editors' killing floor. Poetry about the *peculiar institution* (*i.e.* slavery addressed with "special care") could tick-off 14.

potential "vulgarity" and "suggestiveness."

the arm as it pulled awa**A A A A A**a single, spurting sentence of pornography and barbarity.

Middle Passa**KRA A A A** ge **A**AK! KRAK!————

a tradition of white artists pursuing innovation through Black and brown bodies as a subject and si————te. } power. commerce. and violent control.

||||

Slaver**F F F F F**Y!!!!!! *Éden Éden Éden*

/ Soldiers, helmets cocked down,
don't —— legs spread **0 0 0 0 0** know
trampling,
muscles
drawn back over new-born
KRAK! babes swad **UU 4H**————w**H**hich
dled in
scarlet,   Lyn**NN NN**ching
violet   g from
sto**0 0 0 0** !!!!!!!-shawls: ba   from from
bies falli| arms of
ne walls   women
oozing   huddled
spattered with brains,

Etymologically,
its title reads
Delightful Place
Delightful Place.

orchards blooming. palm-trees. swoll
en in in in in fire, exploding: flowers, pollen, buds,
grasses, paper, rags spotted with milk, with shit,
KRAK!   with blood…

Which ones would be gratuitous?

139

Coste Lewis

On Rachel Zucker's podcast,
Commonplace, Robin Coste
Lewis remarks:
Beauty is a dark, heinous, sublime,
awe-inspiring thing
… Black, strong, iron, unapologetic.
Beauty is a dark, heinous, sublime,
awe-inspiring thing
… Black, strong, iron, unapologetic.

Beauty is a dark, heinous, sublime,
awe-inspiring Black, strong, iron,
   sublime,   heinous dark, Beauty
strong, unapologetic. dark,
awe-inspiring iron Black, thing

Beauty is a strong, dark,
heinous Black, unapologetic.
Black, dark, awe-inspiring thing

Beauty is a strong, iron dark, Black, awe-inspiring
   sublime, heinous a unapologetic. thing

horrified by such beautiful craft.

Johnson   Johnson   Burroughs

A lynching is a performance. AAAAA An act of site-specific theater.

Lynchings have pla A ed AAAAI||||FFFEE I'm not making metaphor.
But they cried out, saying: before crowds large and small. And when the troupe hears crickets and
not whoops of approval. the show tends to go on. w|||| Ithout sweet talk or mystery.
Crucify him! -   See FFFFF!!!!! how the skin begins to gather !!!!! at his ankles,
Crucify him!   how it sli
The ones being lynched are triple threats: they are the stars, the props, and snack bar.
In "Black —— our head OOOOO into ovation. I'm not making metaphor.
Memorabilia," CM Burroughs Crucify him! works the precarious frisson
Amaud Jamaul Johnson's UU HH ters around a lynched man HH the tension move
"Burlesque". how flame fingers each button, of pain and sensuality I let through me
They dressed him up in a purple robe, with violence and e N ntertainment, too. Try not to scream.
I'm n N N Not making metaphor.
olls back his collar, unzips him is up the embers, how it shimmers   blood be
And they pressed it down —   beneath him, unshapen,   blood be
                                  iridescent,   blood be on
Yet, Johnson writes with c OOOO ||| ld irony at metaphor,   on
Oh, they
suc And they mocked my sweet King Je sus ine
—— how his whole body becomes song...
the deep figures of his restaging as symmetrical consideration,
not poetic substitutions.

               I wonder whether it's
                I wonder whether
           whether it's
                it's
Watch the fire undress,   See how the skin begins to gather
how flame fingers each button, at ___ ankles, how it slips into
rolls back ___ collar, unzips ___   the embers, how it shimmers
without sweet talk or mystery. it's beneath ___ , unshapen, iridescent,

        ... how ___ whole body becomes song...
                I
                I
        I'm not making metaphor.

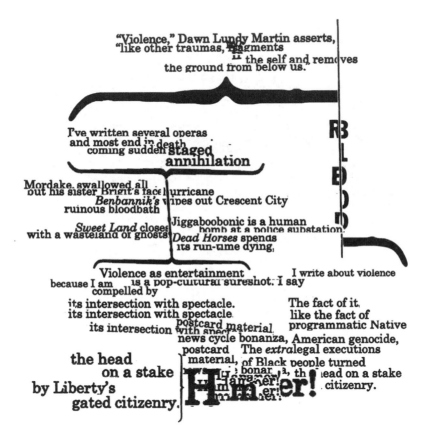

"Violence," Dawn Lundy Martin asserts,
"like other traumas, fragments
the self and removes
the ground from below us."

RBLED
LOOD

I've written several operas
and most end in death
coming suddenly **staged**
annihilation

Mordake. swallowed all
out his sister Brigit's face Hurricane
Benbannik's wipes out Crescent City
ruinous bloodbath

Sweet Land closes Jiggaboobonic is a human
with a wasteland of ghosts bomb at a police substation.
Dead Horses spends
its run-time dying.

Violence as entertainment   I write about violence
because I am   is a pop-cultural sureshot. I say
compelled by

its intersection with spectacle.   The fact of it.
its intersection with spectacle.   like the fact of
its intersection with spec postcard material.   programmatic Native
news cycle bonanza,   American genocide,
postcard   The *extra*legal executions
the head   material, of Black people turned
on a stake   bonar   a, the head on a stake
by Liberty's   Hammer!   citizenry.
gated citizenry.

142

The fact of it, **fills my mind,**
Another fact. There is blood. my pages,

I type the word *blood*. Type it again.
Type it again.
Type it again.
Type it again.
Type it again.
Type it again.

My exhausted imagination a
welter of red, red, red.

Blood soaks through paper.

"Hold on, the bear still needs its fancy cane."

I KILLED, I DIED

BANTER, SELF-DESTRUCTION, AND THE POETRY READING

For Hope Kearney, Amaud Jamaul Johnson, the Black Took Collective, Tisa Bryant, Lillian-Yvonne Bertram, Gabrielle Civil, Jonah Mixon-Webster, and dancing bears everywhere

This lecture about water bottles and what their labels say re: triangular trades.

This lecture about appetizer platters, gouda cooling, un-Tobied, in Baton Rouge rooms.

This lecture about being funny. Funny at poetry readings.

This lecture about Nina Simone's mojowork and the Black Took Collective's collective shade.

This lecture about an eight-inch-thick, award-winning concrete wall in Tucson.

This lecture about how to be reading poetry at poetry readings is to be being funny.

This lecture about dancing bears and the sad way one funny man said "book."

This lecture about the tripartite poetry reading ecosystem, where the *n* in *econ* is silent, especially when the N_____s is not.

This lecture about how revealing what one's fixed to begin often falls between an ending and "this next one" at a poetry reading, and how funny it can be to find yourself, there, banked before and betwixt poems. Let's call that space of potential revelation an interstice. And when one acts into it, let's call it: banter.

And by way of that banter, you mean to reveal something more about what you've revealed in the poem itself, which is why you're where you are. Before something. Betwixt others.

Say you feel your poem says it all, maybe you say nothing, save:
"This one's called—"
And if you feel your poem says it all, maybe you still say something more.
"My blood type is ____. Here, now, is my blood."
Let's call that funny.
This lecture about how when I say funny I mean like telling jokes:

Why did the chicken cross the road?

And this lecture about how when I say funny like telling jokes, I also mean:

Why did the poet keep reading poems about a miscarriage?

And funny like:

Why did the audience clap?

And this lecture about how to be funny funny funny reading poetry at a poetry reading somewhere. So: as the applause frittered, this poet quipped:

It's okay to clap. The baby would have been Black.
My next poem is called—

This lecture about trash barrels on wheels, full of strangers' garbage.
This lecture about a poem what makes this poet gag onstage.
This lecture about a miscarriage.
This lecture's going to be funny as all hell.
This one's called:
"I Killed, I Died."

Being funny at poetry readings is easy because poetry readings are already funny.

Lesson one: show up at poetry reading and read poetry.

You hi*lar*ious.

This lecture's called "I Killed, I Died." But it's called more than that, otherwise you may not know what I'm fixed to begin.

In stand-up comic argot, some say to die is to have a shit set. You perform seeking laughter, yet get none. Conversely, to kill is to work a great set: the crowd reacts exactly as you'd have them. In this rhetorical order, being funny smacks of combat. I offer that the "funny" what doesn't mean joke, but "funny" as in an effed-up dynamic, the ill feel below many poetry readings, is also ontologically violent. That violence comes up without even having to dredge a masculinist grammar, à la comedian Cristina Ouch, who marked that US stand-up been rooted in white guyness since Twain. Trust, a bit on ontological violence kinda sorta coming soon, but patience: the bear is not yet in its rumpled tutu.

All this to say, the violence folded in this lecture's title is not baggage; that is, it needs no sly unpacking. Still, the subtitle, falling there between it and the lecture, opens the bag.

This lecture about:

What happens at the reading when we come to unpack what we think we packed in the poem and find the poetry reading itself is just another bag.

Only, a trick bag.

This lecture is called: "I Killed, I Died: Banter, Self-Destruction, and the Poetry Reading."

A joke:

> What do you call it when people who can probably read come to
> an event to attend other people reading what they've often already
> read?

But seriously, folx. Let me tell you about this one time in Tucson at the
University of Arizona's Poetry Center for the Poetry Off the Page sym-
posium. That was 2012; but for years prior, my wife, Nicole, and I were
a heterosexist white supremacist's dream come true: a Black woman
and man who only fucked each other but were infertile!

That's called killing two crows with bum bones.

> "Haaaaaaaaaamburger!"[1]

I was doing these poems about the miscarriage of who would have been
our firstborn child. A girl. We had tried and tried—IUI: intrauterine
insemination. Turkey baster. It took! But then, the baby girl was taken.
Nicole named her Hope. All I could think was: we lost her.

> "Daaaaaaaaaaaaamn!"[2]

You know, folx, writing these poems took more than a little bit. I tried
and tried. The miscarriage was in 2008. But, in 2011, the process finally
bore fruit after many failed attempts. Which seems terribly appropri-
ate.

> "I ain't scared of you muthafuckas!"[3]

1. Shout-out to comedian Alonzo "Hamburger" Jones.
2. Shout-out to comedian Chris Tucker.
3. Shout-out to comedian Bernie Mac.

Banter works like this. You speak to the audience before you begin the poem. This actually could be about anything, but most often you open the poem up for the audience. A vivisection of sorts, but, we were using a baggage image system—and don't let me be misunderstood. Perhaps you describe how the poem came to be, what motivated you to write it. A fact at its heart and how you came by it. Perhaps there's a craft matter to make plain. A prosodic schema. An allusion.

Yet, why come all this?

Is it your awareness that in the time it takes to read the poem live, vital information might breeze past? Banter, you figure, tethers the poem against that. You reckon, perhaps, if a poem isn't itself precisely narrative, it might need a membrane of story to resonate in communal space. You might also be flexing. Oh yes, flexing. Perhaps there's a lit-crit, pedagogical moment. You wish to prove that you are serious, that you have done work, even when that work—and its attendant serious-ness—might not be apparent in the elusive passage of the poem. Pos-sibly, you suspect your poem is "difficult" and you seek—via anecdote, explanation, or prolepsis—to make it "easier," lest you die up there, ric-tus slick with flop sweat.

And maybe—for know that "and" not "or" is a default in killing and dying's context—you'd like to be funny. For one way to gauge engage-ment is by laughter when you'd have it. Funny while feeling funny in the funny situation of a poetry reading.

What wasn't funny, but funny, and a little funny, was during the three years of writing miscarriage poems that themselves didn't work, I had been working at writing a poem that would make the reader hurt as much as I had.

That poem would've killed!

The impulse guiding that poem reminds me of something from Maggie Nelson's *The Art of Cruelty*, a Mike Kelley quote: "I make art to give other people my problems." Instead, "Miscarriages" were the sum of the takeaway that I couldn't, then shouldn't, make anyone feel what I had felt. And why? I would love to say that it would be to avoid cruelty, but you'll see, if you haven't yet, that ship sailed, that ship sank. Rather, it would place Hope in deepening circles of precarity to have her loss cut by larger catastrophes, binning her to a tchotchke in trauma's marketplace. Funny funny funny.

The miscarriage poem became, instead, a series of poems using an approach similar to another poem about horror—private, public, local, and global catastrophe, "Swimchant for Nigger Mer-Folk," my peppy poem about the Middle Passage. Pep AND horror. No *or*.

But this is not a lecture about poems! This is a lecture about "Banter, Self-Destruction, and the Poetry Reading"—and I'll tell you about poems, yes, because that's what the banter was and sometimes still is for me. So:

At first, I meant to hurt the reader as I hurt losing my daughter. I learned I couldn't and shouldn't do that. Instead: I made the poems funny.

"The Miscarriage: A List of 10 Euphemisms for Use in Stage Banter."

foxes looted the coop!

God marked your copy!

4. Shout-out to comedian Jimmy Durante.

cherries dammed the flume!

a kite fell in April!

an apple burst the nest!

some Seminoles fled the field!

our wagon crashed but we just saw the heart in the furrow!

four alarm beat three days ago and next the doll factory!

roses week is Father's Day choke the cabbage!

red ants blitz the sugar bowl!

The University of Arizona's Poetry Center has the Poetry Off the Page gig archived. Watching the video, I see I opened with an early draft of "The Miscarriage: A Magic Trick." And though I have, on occasion, written bulleted notes at the tops of poems—dates to keep straight, people to attribute—the banter, here, comes off ad-libbed. I hadn't decided what to read before taking the mic; I was riffing, riffling pages for the poems at the lectern.

When you are on stage and need to fill time, it's called padding.

"I'm going to begin—um with—uh—some cheerful poems—um about aaaaahhhh well—miscarriages."

There's a groan.

A titter.

As published in *Patter* (Red Hen Press, 2014), "The Miscarriage: A List of 10 Euphemisms for Use in Stage Banter" is the first poem in a series of seven, most of which I've read over a decade now, but on the regular from 2011 to 2016.

In that time, I've whet the banter to a keener edge.

A wiser poet than I once said you should begin a poetry reading with delight.

"The Miscarriage: A List of 10 Euphemisms for Use in Stage Banter."

After that Tucson reading, the brilliant poet Lillian-Yvonne Bertram approached. They looked a furrowed thoughtful, working something rough over and through, like they do. They said, firmly, yet without rancor, "You are cruel to us." Eight years later, they went further. "Not just the audience. I meant to yourself, too."

Doing the miscarriage series over *Patter*'s cycle, readings grew funnier to me. Poems lit out for the margins of why I'd book a reading, caught up instead with what fell between them.

In this way, this lecture will be, at times, about cruelty. To the audience or to the poet?

There is no *or*.

Another lesson:

Silence is nigh the most frightful thing at a poetry reading. Especially when someone paying you to show.

Banter is "better" than silence, provided you edifying and/or engaging.

But banter's no poem usually, and if you don't poem at the poetry reading, you are not reading poems.

Caveat to the previous statement: "Just read the damn poem!" they may shout. Lots more think this than shout it. Some may generally be fine with banter, but come the hell on.

Many people who detest banter are the poets themselves. "Just listen to the damn poem!" they would shout, or, "Just pay me for writing the damn poem!"

Banter is of unknown etymological origins except that it is reckoned to come from British vernacular during the mid-seventeenth century.

LECTURE!

It is a possible anglicization of the Gaelic term "bean"—meaning "woman"—

LECTURE!

This would LECTURE! suggest that LECTURE! banter bears LECTURE! associations with LECTURE! "women's talk." LECTURE!

People who dislike banter likely don't know this etymology. Mostly, I wager, they want the poem to speak for itself. Which is funny because:

> What do you call it when people who can probably read come to an event to attend other people reading what they've often already read?

It's an inconvenient truth that poets are not always sensitive readers of their own work. Sensitive to all types of shit—including the roomful of people making to listen. Since unlike almost every other spectator event in the US, many poetry readings are spectated by people who, generally, can do the same thing the people in the spotlight can, which is read a poem aloud. Compare this spectacle to watching professional athletes play basketball, trained dancers perform ballet, practiced pop stars in concert. Banter—particularly when it provides insight into process—is a reason why the presence of the poet makes some sense, beyond maybe making cents.

Yet, commerce is but one angle of what most poetry readings triangulate. Edification and engagement, like Avon and Marlo, hold their corners down, too.

The first, edification—it is good for us to be assembled together, and to gather for poetry is even better! We will get cultured, educated, incited to be something more than what we were. This promise lubricates as it imbricates the next.

Commerce, why, don't you look ravishing? Capital will change hands. A cover charge? Books, merch, refreshments sold? The venue may attract patrons via the poets it invites—the academic institution's visiting artist list or the cultural center's seasonal collateral. Reputation vis-à-vis the roster becomes capital.

We've goods that are good for you. But are they good to you?

Thus, engagement. That poetry is beloved by organizers of poetry readings does not preclude its instrumentalization. Many a soul singer tips love and being used on a scale of mutual pleasure. Such tilt may feel uncomfortable here, as poetry, being underfunded, in capitalist love language is therefore underappreciated. The inverse is that in po-biz's nominally anti-capitalist ethos, this disinterest makes it appreciate more. Therefore, even edification is a bourgeois anti-spice, a tote-bagging of poetry into an overpriced, organic supraconsumable.

Mea culpa: triangulating trades do the most to me by their ruthless drive at meaning to turn some beauty into more ugly, and should you believe in that route as an inherent, immutable contamination, there's some other shit we must talk dirty about.

Besides, I didn't pack my baggage, leave my private residence, get TSA'd, fly coach, come to Tucson or wherever, and get in these lecture halls or multipurpose rooms or coffee shops or art galleries or street festivals or libraries or conference rooms or museums or parks or living rooms or historic homes or cultural centers or auditoriums or recording studios or classrooms or black boxes to not have my trauma remembered.

Hold on: the bear still needs its fancy cane.

This one's called: "Amaud Jamaul Johnson knows what's up."

When we are writing about pain, what is banter? Awkward-ass jokes? Trigger warnings? What does it mean when we're triggered by our own work?

AMAUD JAMAUL JOHNSON

Reading the "Miscarriage" poems over and over made readings feel funnier than usual.

What had happened was I grew more and more angry. With myself first, for writing the poems. Then for reading them, for using them to kill audiences.

So, I altered my banter, to play it straight, to unpack—but the incongruity between the poems' tone and disclosure made me feel cheap, there before the audience sharing grief and then doing a magic trick, a minstrel show, a bar joke. This made the poems appear, at best, cathartic—we can all laugh now—and they weren't. They aren't. They may numb me, a kind of dying, a kind of killing. But they relieve nothing for me but a compositional problem.

Banter serves, too, as a compositional problem when seen in a structural relationship to the poem it precedes and, sometimes, follows.

I had used banter as many do, as a guard against the audience turning on me. I still wanted to kill and not die, like a comic. And, to a comic, to have an audience turn on you is when a joke makes them dislike you in a way you don't mean to mean.

To "turn on you" suggests, in comedy, betrayal.

In poetry, however, it suggests a volta.

With *Patter*, was I who turned on the audience.

In comedian Christopher Titus's 2017 special, *Born with a Defect*, right around 45:57, he self-interrupts a characteristically twisted bit with what sounds like a bantered aside:

> I've gotten to a very sick place with comedy, I've done this so long now—this is my seventh special—I want you guys to know something. So: I want you guys to laugh. And I'm used to that, I've been doing that a long time. Now I've gotten to this weird place like a guy who's had way too much sex where I need it a little weird. So, I'll write a joke . . . where you guys go—ha-ha-ha—oh-ooohhh.

Titus mimics a spectator's game laughter, before abruptly pulling a look of their dawning dismay; then, Titus is Titus again, doing a victory gesture that reads: I'm getting off.

Note the disclosure of his joke-writing process. Next, pausing for this aside creates an interstice that he fills with the banter's tricky metacommentary.

My wife and I have dug Titus's stand-up for a minute. Met him in a Target, back in California when we lived in the Valley—waaaaaay before *Born with a Defect*. This would have been around the time of the miscarriage.

We would have seen *Norman Rockwell Is Bleeding* (2004) at that point. That's the one where Titus is building a bookcase, and this sets his girlfriend off! Explaining why he's building it, Titus says—"Book" —his mouth falling open like a bladder emptying itself.

It's terrible, the fear in it. The sense of imminent failure. His trauma was material—abusive relationships, an alcoholic parent, another parent with a mental illness. Can't say whether his shows were cathartic. But we thought they were hilarious and painful.

In Target, he was shucks over our low-key yet earnest compliments. Still, he looked startled at first. Dismay abruptly pulling into dawning laughter.

The crowd howls after his confession and pantomime in *Born with a Defect*. "I know, I know." He says, shuddering off the illicit pleasure, returning to the act, "I have a problem. It's not good."

He's killing them!

The thing, though. When the bit within the bit started? When the audience groaned their dismay? Titus was laughing. Nearly the only one laughing at an awkward-ass joke. Was that dying? Or, did he want their buttoned silence—thus, killing?

"OR" has no place with the funny I am talking about. This messy funny too much many.

I'm about to talk about banter and self-destruction. My studies in banter and self-destruction are, however, accelerations of the latent negation implicit in banter at a poetry reading. LECTURE! Banter facilitates a dialogic relation between the poet and the audience; yet this is false: the poet speaks to the audience as auditor. LECTURE! Rather than seeing this as the poet given essential "power" in the context of the reading, the triangular exchange structure described above posits the terms of power are administrated through commerce. LECTURE!—

What I'm saying is, even though it looks like the poet is in power because the poet is the one with the mic, the option not to speak is actually the sign of power. The poet in characteristic US American readings is the "object" and "consumable" of the reading, the product/service. Their utterance is a site to be judged—by the audience, not a site that exacts power or generates law over the audience. The conventions of the poetry reading are the source of order. The audience's option to "utter," then, becomes a mapping of their *krisi-critico*[5] engagement and evaluation of the poet's compulsory "utterance." This is an activity of judgment, anti-spiced as "appreciation." Banter accommodates and expedites this *krisi-critico* function by laying bare/breaking down (stripping and taking apart) the poem as a site of motivations and procedurals for the poet. Thus, the poet takes on the conflicting roles of witness/criminal, debunker/magician, craftsperson/seer, critic/artist—as prolepsis, a preemptive defense against or accommodation for the audience's evaluation. These pairings are kept as "OR" conditions by the shored border between "banter" and "poem"—"Now," the poet seems to say, "I am a witness to the crime of the poem. Here's how it was done."

"This crime's called—"

LECTURE!

LECTURE!

5. To suggest judgment (decision/accusation) and criticality.

LECTURE!

LECTURE!

Should this lecture be called: "I Killed, I Died: Banter, *Self-Snitching*, and the Poetry Reading"? I've no side-eye for confession. Besides, what the listed pairs—witness/criminal, debunker/magician, craftsperson/seer, critic/artist—come to get at isn't snitching; they undo each other. They headed for self-destruction—the slash a typographic wound at an epistemological crime scene.

What I'm here to report is that I've meant to excise that slash. Not in my bio, my artist statements, but at my readings themselves.

Recall the proffered structure—banter, poem, banter, poem, banter, poem?

Then, the notion of volta—a turn, marking a change?

Here's the volta in my poetry-reading praxis. I no longer put a slash between banter and poem. In fact, the reading has become a site in which I attempt to reproduce the associative space of poetic composition publicly.

The results have been funny.

I've a habit of laughing at my own jokes. The sound goes "ts." An almost shame.

My son does it, too.

I think it's because if I try to be funny, I'm trying because of anxiety. A desire to please.

I rarely laugh at my own jokes during my banter.

Once, though, it struck me to do so. I was reading at a library in Hudson.

A quick note on structure versus form. In a poem, structure speaks to the cognitive path the poem takes. Image to question? Past to present to shitty epiphany?

Form recommends how many and what kind. How many lines, syllables? How many rhymes? How many repetitions? What kind of syllables and in what kind of sequence? And so on.

Back in Hudson, I was in the middle of banter, riffing, and it happened that what I said had the structure of a joke. In that instant, I decided to laugh. Rather, bark out the form of a laugh. A mirthless laughter about how painting sidewalks green in gentrifying neighborhoods would make it easier to edit cops out of their own police brutality selfie vids. Something terribly not funny, but funny. This made the reading even funnier.

The structure of a joke—as comedian Hannah Gadsby puts it—is two parts: setup and punch line. The setup, she asserts, is a question, the answer for which—the punch line—is a surprise. For Gadsby, many of these questions are "artificially inseminated" with tension.

I make you all feel tense, and then I make you laugh, and you're like, "Thanks for that. I was feeling a bit tense." *I* made you tense. *This* is an abusive relationship!

She continues:

Do you know why I'm such a funny fucker? Do you? It's because, you know, I've been learning the art of tension diffusion since I was a children [*sic*]. Back then it wasn't a job, wasn't even a hobby, it was a survival tactic. I didn't have to invent the tension. I was the tension. And . . . I'm tired of tension. Tension is making me sick.

That the poetry reading is funny

funny

funny

doesn't make it stand-up. Yet the funniness is a source of tension. Banter, by presencing the poet (I'm here to tell you about the poem and not just read it to you), is meant to ease one funny tension (the poet's reading may not help us appreciate the poem as an autonomous, aesthetic object) yet activates several more, like:

—edification with a desire to dismiss a language of instrumentalization

—an engagement of judgment

—a series of self-undoing gambits on the poet's part

The banter is there to help the audience get the poem (like a riddle, not a joke) and for the poem to be got (like a gift, not a baby). If we note incidental tension in banter, it is often when something goes wrong. And this wrongness also alerts us to the structure of the poetry reading itself—why don't they just read the poem?—spurred by discomfort, impatience, *fremdschämen*, and more.

Gadsby constructs an argument about joke structure as a binary—question and answer—with artificial insemination as a delivery mode for an abusive relationship between herself and the audience. This allows a slick critique of gender normativity and sets up *Nanette*'s punch line, Gadsby's ready to quit comedy. A joke's two parts stick her stuck in trauma and tension, but story allows a third bit. An ending. The laugh, she says, precludes the possibility of resolution.

After *Nanette*, Gadsby doesn't end her relationship with comedy. Her follow-up, released in 2020, is called *Douglas*.

If I were to adopt Gadsby's structural critiques as tactics, I'd get at how poems need not set up anything, answer anything, nor resolve in the way we understand a narrative or rhetorical progress tromping doggedly along. People may prefer poems generally that do some combination or singularity of all of these. Some may come to love them a poem—and be surprised they do—when it does any of these things in any combination or isolation. That hill's no stage I mean to kill or die on.

This lecture about: "Banter, Self-Destruction, and the Poetry Reading."

In Hudson, what I was setting up was a joke that had already been told. And I was nearly the only one laughing.

I had already died. And all I could do was keep dying till it killed.

"What does it mean when we're triggered by our own work?"

Ha! Ha! Ha!   Ha! Ha! Ha!   Ha! Ha! Ha!   Ha! Ha! Ha!

When a performer laughs at the wrong time during an act or scene, it's called "corpsing." Which, in theater, specifically describes an actor who can't stop laughing when their character is meant to be serious, played straight, or, as some report being how the term originates: dead. YouTube's got lots of compilations of cast members corpsing in *Saturday Night Live* sketches. They throwing the tension away like zoooong! Often to mask corpsing, actors will bury their faces in their hands, a pose similar to weeping. I suppose this is crying to keep from laughing. The precise inverse of what I was taught signifying does.

The bear nearly has its tap shoes on.

When I laughed that laugh that wasn't laughter at something that was funny thus not FUNNY funny, I was not laughing to keep from crying. Rather, like tense banter, I hoped to see a structure. To disclose. Not, however, the poems I had packed; instead, the arrangement that had brought me packing and packed the audience in. I ain't Carver this peanut. You can find it in Brecht and in BAM, in punk and in Piper, and, by and by, the Black Took Collective and Nina Simone.

At the same time, in Hudson and elsewhere, I didn't plan to do what I did. I just didn't stop myself from doing what occurred to me under the circumstances. This is very similar to where I try to be when I'm writing. I follow an association, put a line down, move a collaged piece of text between two others, and half bury a fourth. Then, from that move, I make the next, hoping to synthesize the smaller gestures into something shaking with both centrifugal and centripetal energy.

With this new banter, composition includes my body, my acoustic voice, the room and its contents, the poems, and the audience. Yet, I am not composing a new poem but refining a lifelong poetics—my body, observed in a space. I'm a professional at that.

Professionalism, as a convention of disciplinary discipline, is eschewed first in this new banter. Rassling a bottle of water on the floor in Alabama is, I suppose, another kind of self-destruction. A risk inherent in pursuing the associative in real-time in real life.

Put finer: I don't know what I'm going to do. Which means neither does the venue. *Nota bene*: not knowing what I'm about to do isn't the same as not knowing what I'm about. The improvisational aspect of the banter ghosts my sense of time while simultaneously keeping me on time. This decenters the composed poem(s) with what plays like an uncomposed act of performative riffing. It isn't composed (prewritten), but it is composed—in the sense that it is self-possessed.

As Arthur Jafa puts it:

> Classically, jazz improvisation is first and foremost signified self-determination. This actually precedes its function as musical gesture. For the black artist to stand before an audience, often white, and to publicly demonstrate her decision-making capacity, her agency, rather than the replication of another's agency, i.e., the composers, was a profoundly radical and dissonant gesture. . . . This signification of one's "self-determination" is in turn premised on one's "selfpossession." There is no "self-determination" without "self-possession." And, "self-possession" is *the* existential issue for black Americans.
>
> ARTHUR JAFA, from "My Black Death"

I may die. I do not corpse.

On architecture. The Poetry Center in Tucson was designed by architect Les Wallach, FAIA of Line and Space, LLC. "The University of Arizona Poetry Center," the studio's website reads, "one of the first and only buildings on any university campus dedicated solely to celebrating and advancing poetry and literature." To meet that cause, Line and Space designed structures allowing for natural light while minimizing the collection's exposure to the sun's paper-hungry ultraviolet rays.

Such are the tensions what drive the award-winning building's story. Isabelle Lomholt, writing for the UK's e-architect website, notes the center's knotty needs—light to read by, but not too bright. Intimacy, despite ginormous holdings, functional accessibility, and ready security. These contradictions seem fit to me as principles of a house housing poetry.

Upon first visiting for the Poetry Off the Page symposium, I was guided through the center's library. There, I saw slanted glass and honeyed wood, eastern garden views backed by the featured "binary wall"—whose apertures light the bambooed refuge and, via shaded glass, the collection stacks, while reproducing Richard Shelton's passage ". . . I will learn the art of silence" in binary code. I found it beautiful.

Lomholt writes,

The connection between reader and poetry are overarching in the Poetry Center's design and is refined in the plan of the building which is conceived as a "progression towards solitude." Progression starts at the west with an active and noisy Humanities Seminar Room whose transparent walls can be opened, allowing flexibility within the shaded transition space, and doubling the seating capacity for larger events.

The last time I was at the Poetry Center was in 2017 for the Thinking Its Presence conference, founded by Prageeta Sharma. I was in a keynote collaboration called "Fodder," with the pulled-up musician Val Jeanty[6], in the Humanities Seminar Room. The transparent walls flung wide, chairs spoked out from Val's turntables with aisles like rays dividing the larger seating sections. We were in our set, about to do a poem called "Runaway Tongue." I remember looking over at Val—she was cueing something—another couple of seconds? Bet. We needed some padding just like the first time I was in the Humanities Seminar Room back in 2012, looking for the "Miscarriage" poems' terrible magic.

"Runaway Tongue" is at the kid's table in a banquet set by Harryette Mullen's poetry and critical work[7], along with ideas about fugitivity. Peppered throughout the poem's open field is the phrase "Get it." I said before, that could suggest a joke told, but here, also: a code caught, something escaped.

But I didn't say any of that on October 20, 2017. Instead, to explain the poem, I ran.

Lomholt writes of the Poetry Center, "Moving east, public functions dissolve into more intimate spaces within the collection—one finds themselves in the bamboo garden, an outdoor area of solitude and contemplation."

6. Ayibòbò!

7. Namely, *"Runaway Tongue: Resistant Orality in Uncle Tom's Cabin, Our Nig, Incidents in the Life of a Slave Girl,* and *Beloved."*

My "moving east" was a fifty-foot sprint from the Humanities Seminar Room toward the library's wall of concrete masonry laid in a stack bond pattern. This smooth, gray surface—eight inches thick—is what I ran into.

And why? If I avoided the wall, there would be no reason to stop running, would there? It would not have made what we could call dramaturgical sense. I figured that out midsprint and prepared to hit the wall.

I jumped some and splayed the flats of my forearms and palms in front of me with some slack, just to absorb the shock. This allowed me to control my torso and thighs as they clapped into the concrete. The grace note? My glasses somersaulting from my face, clattering to the ground. I followed.

But what then? My escape had been blocked. If I went to the left, there was an open parking lot, and I'd be back to the situation in which I'd have to just keep running. If I slunk back to the stage, running would have been rhymeless, a thorn line. So, I looked to the right, and there— reddish, orange—a guardrail. I ran smack at that and found it, thankfully, securely bolted to the ground.

Now my poetics had a form and a structure.

I ran back toward the seminar room, slamming into the merch table. Then, the last leg of the square route, I headed to the stage, a tongue returned to work at the mic. Turns out, this direction, the same direction as the parking lot I saw after the first wall?

North.

Sometimes poems do things we don't intend. And if one's banter becomes a kind of poem-making, the same applies.

Improvisation creates opportunities and misses others.

I ran at LSU earlier that year. Not because of "Runaway Tongue." I can't remember why, honestly. Had I run through the audience into the reception area, I would have seen several platters of hors d'oeuvres. I promise you, I would have grabbed one of those platters, returned to that grand room in Baton Rouge, and begun serving the guests.

Sadly, I ran behind the staging area. I, too, was confused.

With the wall, the self-destruction was immediate and physical. At LSU, running away from the stage seemed random, unprofessional, and impulsive. What would the gesture of carrying the tray have been? Presencing a racial history in the context of giving a reading in the grand, old room. Gadsby, who self-identifies as a gender nonconforming lesbian, argues that for people from historically oppressed identities, self-deprecating humor isn't humility but humiliation.

What, however, when it's not FUNNY but funny?

Introducing the dancing bear!

The "dancing bear" is an intervention formulated by Tisa Bryant after reading Aimé Césaire, who, in *Notebook of a Return to My Native Land*, writes: "A man screaming is not a dancing bear. Life is not a spectacle." She connects this to:

> [t]he numerous anecdotes from Black women writers, from Octavia Butler to Gayl Jones to Toni Morrison to Toni Cade Bambara, in which a teacher doubts that the Black schoolgirl indeed wrote the short story submitted for the grade, because such intellectual ability cannot belong to Black girls; such intellectual ability is not believed to be organic.

On spectacle, she goes further:

> "Dancing bear" is a spectacle, and perceived as spectacular, on the part of the bear, not as unethical or as torture, on the part of the person hold-

ing the leash and the lash. . . . "Dancing bear" is also a metaphor for the spectacle of Black people, often men, being human and excelling in a field that racists perceive as being beyond a Black person's ken. Said Black person is seen as exceptional, wondrous entertainment, and the spectre of the trainer, with leash and lash, operates in the racist imaginary, and is often conflated with the spectator themselves.[8]

Y'all know something? My grandfather on my father's side used to wrestle bears in a circus? Where, Bryant notes, "dancing bears" were "real fodder"?

When I'm at a poetry reading, I feel like the bear and the person there to wrestle it.

If the bear wins, what happens to the human wrestler? If the human wrestler wins, what becomes of the bear? Is the leash just a lash that lashes to instead of at? Does the one who holds the leash discipline both the bear and the human wrestler? Can that person take the bear and wrestler on?

Would negrotesquely serving little shrimps on toasts between reading poems also make me the person holding the leash, the lash?

No OR! No OR! No OR!

I feel bound to whip up this kind of trouble—my thinking on the potential to destabilize the poetry reading with something less self-destructive is indebted, as Bryant is, to a line before me. But in the time I've left, I'll call the Black Took Collective and Nina Simone to offer strategies for study.

8. Though Bryant notes the gendering of "dancing bear," she asserts its fluidity further down in the passage: "The Black schoolgirl is a dancing bear cub, not real, a trick, temporary, a cheat, plagiarism, using a greater power, e.g., the white trainer."

Poking the "dancing bear" trope seemed something the Black Took Collective was particularly into. Duriel E. Harris, Dawn Lundy Martin, and Ronaldo V. Wilson's use of masks, multimedia, discursive engagement with minstrelsy—in Tin Pan Alley and the Ivory Tower—are interventions, queer, negrotesque, heated, and funky, monkey wrenches into what Bryant calls "the persistent doubting of ability, originality, motivation, innovation, dignity and distinction, Black people contend with daily." I saw them off-site at the same Poetry Off the Page symposium I attended. They typed live, projecting text onto screens flanking the stage. We, the audience, came to realize the Collective was transcribing fragments of our conversations, things the Collective overheard as we filed into the auditorium, phrases they recalled from panel presentations, decontextualized into their performance.

As the Collective typed, Harris, Martin, and Wilson disregarded the performer's convention of giving face to the crowd; instead, they turned away, hunched at their screens. Typing, they read, but rather than the feeling of a poetry reading, the recital was like a court record presented, especially if your part came up. The *krisi-critico* function script flipped on the spectator, leashed into the spotlight.

Some members of the audience laughed to see and hear fragments of their own conversations blown up, their voices as text, displayed as show, *the* show. Many were dismayed by the effect of this reversal, a violation of semi-private speech. Such a move can be harrowing for an audience member; in fact, one explained to the Black Took Collective that their provocation and its arc of nonconsensual disclosure triggered memory of a sexual assault. There is, as the Collective knows, cruelty in such work.

The Collective's real-time process was metacommentary without an aside, a kind of crowd-work that worked with their own crowded stage. Harris/Martin/Wilson's distinct styles might suggest a variety show, and sure, the rupture of a poetry reading was the starting principle, informed as they are by Erica Hunt's "Notes for an Oppositional Poetics." But in action was a poetics that, unlike banter's urge to break down or a poem's fate to metonymize, created excess out of the structural bric-a-brac of the reading. If one is to be consumed, rapper Method Man says: "I'll sew your asshole closed and keep feeding you and feeding you and feeding you and feeding you . . ."

Nina Simone, Malik Gaines observes, deploys "three distinct elements of her mode of performance: her intertextual material, her shamanistic technique, and her theatrical presentation." Locating centrally the spells she casts operates for me as the linchpin of a possible banter corrective. As Gaines notes, "In Simone's oeuvre, anecdotes abound of her scolding her audiences, appearing late, and other divalike behaviors." The cost of these acts in her acts thrusts us back into the edification/commerce/engagement triangle.

For the engagement to be on Simone's terms is difficult to parse without reckoning engagement as combat. Simone's iconic banter on "Mississippi Goddam" ("This is a show tune, but the show hasn't been written for it yet") is a languid-seeming threat, with the show ambiguous as a metaphor for coming conflict or the white-washed dismemory of it, retuned for show. It plays metacommentary for a work in progress, a work Simone puts work in on and is working on in the moment of performance. In that way, it discloses, but it discloses that which is unfinished, that which is open and uncloseable. A feint. The banter gives nothing away and, in its irony, relieves perhaps only Simone. One could argue that here is the same Simone persona as in "Pirate Jenny" who's seen the black freighter soon come, it's close at hand, goddamn.

But relief? Even temporary? Simone still knows that she, in this concert hall, must be the wind that blows the ship in and the current that heaves it. To recall Amaud Jamaul Johnson's question: "What does it mean when we're triggered by our own work?" What is the calm before the storm when you are the storm as well?

Irony—in banter—is still a presence of self in a concert hall (read: poetry reading). The poem brought you here, but it is not enough, or you would be at home.

Simone as shaman shifts the dynamic, because to put someone under a spell is to engage them with a power that is, actually, not you. A misdirection. To imagine this with the triangular structure I proposed earlier, Simone—or the poet—acts as a shadow curator. The audience comes thinking they are there to attend the poet; the poet, however, refocuses their attention on something else. Many believe this must be "the poems," leading, I'd offer, to thoughtful and intentional decisions about avoiding banter and projecting a neutral-coded reading affect. However, I don't know that most audiences, or poets, go to readings for poems. They may do so for the potential of finding poetry in the reading's triangulation. And that is not the province of poems alone.

Yet the bill will come due. A joke can be a yoke if your grip on it slips. And unsettling one audience is fine. But if it costs you each time, the audience is fresh. You aren't. The destruction accrues. You might be up in Chicago clipping your lip. Telling a joke that's gonna take everyone in this room with you someplace hot. Ramming your body against a banked stage two taller people easily mounted in Boise, Idaho, then dragging yourself around it, a boardless Pope.L, to the stairs upstage, where you claw yourself up there, downstage to the mic, pull yourself up there before saying, "I'm Douglas Kearney."

At that gig, 2019, Boise State University, they gave me bottled water. Which is good, because all that crawling had made me powerful thirsty! It was LIFEWTR.

Uncapping it, I noticed LIFEWTR's brand name is stylized sans the A & E. What a delight! I ad-libbed:

> There's no A and E here, so I guess this is Life Wtrrrrr. Don't worry, I'll provide your A & E for the evening! My people are great with Arts and Entertainment, especially when brought to you by water!

Every so often during the reading, I'd improvise a LIFEWTR/Middle Passage commercial. And at one point, I realized I'd have to pour some on my head. To choose not to would be to be in a poetry reading and its criteria instead of seeing the poetry reading's arrangement and running north for the parking lot. The poems took care of themselves, and I didn't take care of anybody. Not even, I guess, Douglas Kearney.

Which brings us back to funny funny funny. "I Killed, I Died: Banter, Self-Destruction, and the Poetry Reading."

Douglas Kearney has no business at a poetry reading, yet poetry readings are central to the business of poetry. A concern. The pain that concerns so much of my work, reckoning with intimate, biological loss, and social ones may make something happen in a poem. It may consume a poem. It may be all there is. But that poem is not a bottle. It cannot contain any of my pain.

That's what I'm for.

Like you, I show up when that poem being all it is somehow isn't enough. So I come, now, to make poetry. Poetry that includes me and my body, the space and the audience's bodies. Whether that's to tell awkward-ass jokes, give trigger warnings, describe the rhyme scheme, run into concrete masonry, scream till I taste nickels, wheel a recycling receptacle through the audience to collect a dropped iced tea bottle, play the role of dead body at countless murder scenes, have a domestic argument with a book that thuds from a music stand, explain why I did what I did, read the poem like I'm lashing the bear, being lashed, watching it dance, dancing, being grappled and grappling, like I'm trying to kill to keep from dying.

I've seen how this ends if I keep being in this same joke. I saw it the first time I almost puked while reading the poem "Well Hung."

I thought:

> If I throw up, I need to keep going.
> But then there will be vomit on the stage.
> And what, Douglas Kearney, just what will you do with that?

Ha! Ha! Ha!   Ha! Ha! Ha!   Ha! Ha! Ha!   Ha! Ha! Ha!

Ha! Ha! Ha!   Ha! Ha! Ha!   Ha! Ha! Ha!   Ha! Ha! Ha!

Ha! Ha! Ha!   Ha! Ha! Ha!   Ha! Ha! Ha!   Ha! Ha! Ha!

APPENDIX A

THE CAVE CANEM Q&A

"I Killed, I Died: Banter, Self-Destruction, and the Poetry Reading" kicked off my series of Bagley Wright Lectures at an event sponsored by Cave Canem, "the watering hole for Black poetry." This was tremendous for me, as attending Cave Canem from 2000 to 2002 changed the arc of my life.

Here, you'll find a transcript of the Q&A that followed the lecture, moderated by Malcolm H. Tariq. It has been lightly edited for clarity.

MALCOLM TARIQ: Let me try to do this. Great. Wow, thank you for that. I'm going to give you a minute because that was a lot before we go into the Q&A. While we wait, I want to remind people that they can purchase books from Black Garnet, and I will put that link in the chat again. I'd also want to—Let me get this one as well. I also want to tell people that you're going to be at City of Asylum soon, right?

DOUGLAS KEARNEY: Yes.

MALCOLM: You know what day that is?

DOUGLAS: Oh my gosh, that is, I believe it's next Saturday.

MALCOLM: Next Saturday. You're presenting *Tallahatchie Lullabye, Baby* with City of Asylum?

DOUGLAS: Yes. There're going to be several musicians who have been interpreting and responding to that poem. Yes, it's a fantastic, fantastic event, and they're just going to be amazing, I know.

MALCOLM: Yes, definitely. I put that link in our chat. City of Asylum is a longtime partner of Cave Canem. We engage with them every June when we do our retreat in Pennsylvania, right outside of Pittsburgh. Then there's a day when we go into Pittsburgh, and City of Asylum graciously hosts us. We sometimes partner with events now that we are in virtual land. Do please check out Douglas with City of Asylum. They put on awesome events, even virtually, always amazed at that. I know that your event's going to be good. Let's get into some questions, I think. Are you prepared?

DOUGLAS: Yes, I can do that. I can do it, yeah. I can handle it. Thank you on the chat feed. Also, thank you all.

MALCOLM: People were really listening, because there was no activity on the chat while you were talking.

[LAUGHTER]

Oh, I love it. I'm going to ask one of my own questions first while people are still submitting questions. What was the process like for you writing this? You take us through a process, through the lecture, but what was it like for you personally?

DOUGLAS: Gosh. I had originally thought I was going to do a different set of lectures, to be honest. Over the course of the summer, with everything that was going on, I just felt that I wanted to do something a bit more urgent and immediate, knowing that I was going to start with Cave Canem—I said in the beginning, but for real, y'all, I was shook. Shook because this is a place when you come to be bout it, right?

MALCOLM: Yes.

DOUGLAS: The process for it—I wrote down six different titles, just like that immediately came to mind, of things that I would want to work on, that I would want to write about. This was one of them, and I just started working at it. The process moved through a decision about what the tone of it was going to be, how much I felt committed to my assumptions of what the register of a lecture should sound like. I have to say, Ellen [Welcker] told me [the Bagley Wright Foundation] encourage[s] play with the form, break the form.

MALCOLM: Ellen with the Lecture Series?

DOUGLAS: Yes, with the Lecture Series. Thank you. Thank you. I went in at it like that. What I really wanted to figure out was how to talk about this thing that I've been working through a lot recently, which is trying to separate the sense that when I finish a poem, I kinda tuck in my shirt or there's a change, like, "Okay, do the poem." Now, there's a change. I'm now going to introduce this next poem, and now there's going to be another change—but to try to stay in that mode. That was actually one of the guiding principles to the composition of the lecture.

How do I start this with a kind of openness that refuses to falsely separate the idea from an intellectual intelligence, from an emotional intelligence, criticality from the creativity, any of those kinds of things? Don't do that. The ability to fluidly move in and out into different registers became one of the driving principles. When I located the idea of self-destruction as being something that I honestly didn't feel was just a kind of a provocation, just like a provocative thing to put into a title, and then I also began to feel wasn't just about my own work, but was, what is it that we do when we banter at a poetry reading?

It also turned; there was that moment of volta in the lecture as well. There's a way that I really want it to be something, like, to think about and work with. I'm hopeful that it's interesting to people and compelling to people, and something to think about.

MALCOLM: It's definitely very interesting. There's a lot of thought. Thank you. We have a question, this is a good first question. "Can you share further thoughts on the distinctions between poetry and poems?"

DOUGLAS: I would say poetry to me is a set of relations, and possibilities, and responses. You can walk and you can see something that to you becomes a kind of a luminous image. Maybe you're walking by—I was at a White supremacy rally in the Twin Cities in 2001, and there was somebody at the capitol building holding a sign that said something like "White superiority." I'm not making this shit up, and it was upside down. Then somebody must have told him, "Oh, turn it back, upside down." That, to me, was poetry. [CHUCKLES]

That was like poetry, but for me, if I write and describe that, and make it into a poem and render it into something else, that becomes a different possibility. I'm saying this fully aware of a poem like "38," by Layli Long Soldier, when she talks about the Dakota stuffing grass into the mouth of Myrick, like a poem might not need to have words. I'm aware that there might be a kind of cultural freight that I'm bringing into this, but I guess what I want to say is that poetry is something that we can witness, that we can come across, that doesn't require making.

A poem, I feel, is an intervention because poetry, you can look at something and be like, "Oh, look at the sunset or the water hitting this." A poem feels, to me, like a made thing.

I don't think that makes it lesser in a sense of value. I do think, though, that the space that poetry can create encompasses the relation and the responses between potentially a reader of the poem and the writer of the poem, the reader of the poem and the listener or receiver of the poem, if they're not listening, if that's not the mode of reception. To me, poetry can contain that, the poem as the object, or the poem as discrete image.

That, to me, is a distinction that I see, and so the opportunity to create, to be in that associative space where we're all paying attention and aware of that is a kind of notion of poetry.

MALCOLM: Got you, yes. Great. This is from—We have lots of questions now. Kamden Hilliard is asking, "How can we protect ourselves in the act of performance? What kind of rituals before, after have you tried? Can you imagine helpful aftercare for this intimacy?"

DOUGLAS: I was at, I guess it was AWP. Maybe it was Seattle AWP. I can't remember which one; it was a few years ago. I believe it was Rosamond King and Gabrielle Civil were mentioned during a panel they did. Both brilliant poets, performers, artists, thinkers, all of that. These Black women talked about how if they do a reading or a performance, and I'm only putting that "or" there because I can't remember specifically how they described it, they don't do Q&A right after. They're not going to sit down and be like, "Okay, here we are. Here we are to talk."

That's one way for some people to do that. To take that time away to have that moment. The moment you gave me, Malcolm. That moment of, "Okay, let's take a second." That's one way of creating that self-care. That's one way of creating a kind of protection. I have watched people, as a part of their practice, conjure. They draw experience, memory into themselves to manifest. In lots of traditions, there is an infrastructure around the person who becomes the *cheval* to the *loa*. Oftentimes, the poetry reading doesn't have people who are, say, spiritual caretakers to hold people after they do that kind of work. I'm really not saying this with shade; we have applause. We have, "That was amazing." We have, "That was a great job," but again, there's a cultural thing that might be happening in that moment, where a person needs something different.

I think that if you come from a practice where you draw from that, I think it's important to think all the way through the process. How has that process been able to be sustained over time? What are the mechanisms in place? If that's going to be an essential part of your practice as an artist, how can you bring that with you where you go?

If it's not something that you're deeply embedded in as a part of tradition, just be aware of what bits and pieces you draw from because you might not be aware of what it means to call forth certain things into yourself. Like protecting oneself, those are spiritual emotional ways, protecting oneself, but I'll be super mechanical here as well. Physically protecting yourself is important. I used to have a falsetto that was as clear as a bell, but years of yelling and screaming have tore up my voice.

There are things that you have to do in terms of warming up your voice. I know there are people attending this event who have a number of rituals and practices around that. Stuff you can eat, you shouldn't eat anymore, all that kind of stuff. Honey, lemon, tea, that kind of stuff. I think you have to tell yourself, as honestly as you can, why you're there to do what you're doing. When I was first starting to do those poems about our miscarriage, I wasn't always honest with myself about why I was choosing to do these poems. "I'm going to read these poems. I'm going to do this. I'm going to do that."

I don't think you can start the right protection, the right care until you're for real, for real honest about what it is that you want from it. If you go in there, and you're like, "I'm going to do this because I'm third out of six poets, and I want everybody to be like, 'Oh shit, that was incredible, oh my God,'" you need to understand that a part of what is driving you is that kind of an ambition. Does that then mean that you are going to give yourself the space afterwards, to disappear, or are you going to then be like, "All right, I'm ready,

I'm ready, yes, come on, let's chop it up, let's chop it up, keep my name out there"?

I think that those kinds of things, that moment of honesty with yourself is key, and it's just really important.

MALCOLM: I want to remind everybody to put your question in the Q&A box. I forgot to say that at the beginning of the Q&A session, but that's where we're getting the questions from. We're getting a lot of questions and comments about the voice and the body, then some about self-care, or just care in general. I'm going to be pulling from each one of those camps, so we cover the full range. This is from Kameelah Rasheed, who's in the house. "Can you expand a bit more about the difference between structure and form?" They're interested in what you were saying about one being the suggestive, and what suggestive means as poetry builds a relationship with the reader.

DOUGLAS: Okay, all right. This is one of my little favorite thought experiments here. A "simple" way to understand form, the way I think about it, is how much and what kind? Oftentimes, this is something that is perceivable through—and again, I don't mean this negatively—either a cosmetic, or a mechanical, or for a sensate means, like the sensual world. You understand it? Like, a sonnet has this many lines. How many lines? This many. What kind of lines? Usually, this meter. What's the pattern? How are these lines? What's the rhyme this time and this time?

How many rhymes we have? We're going to have this many rhymes. We going to have this. How much, what kind?

Structure, I would argue, is the ideational path that the writing takes. For example, if you watch an interview between a hostile interview subject and a journalist, the interview has a form: question-answer, question-answer. But the structure of that interview might be curiosity, avoidance, deflection, calm, aggression, combat. That's the ideational structure. That's the path of it.

For me, I feel like what happens, when I talk to a lot of poets who are either in my classes or I begin to think this for myself, is that poets are often very good at changing forms and trying new forms. We'll try a new form, but oftentimes we write with the same structure. We write, we go, we start with a memory. Then, we'll do a kind of commenting on that memory. Then, we'll bring that memory into the present, and then we'll have an epiphany. That structure will be present in every poem. Whether it's a tight, little four-line number or a sprawling open field poem, the structure of it moves in the same way ideationally.

I think that's what happens usually when poets feel like they're not generatively writing, they're writing the same thing over and over again. I think anybody who knows anything about my work knows that repetition is not a problem to me. When it's not generative, that, to me, becomes the question, right? For me, one of the experiments I have a student do is, I ask them to come analyze what's the structure, your typical structure. Let's say this is a poet who is oftentimes looking for that epiphany to come in that last line. I'll say, "Okay, there you got your epiphany. Let's make that your second line. Where do you go now? If you don't presume that the poem's structural purpose is to end with epiphany, why does the poem keep going?"

That's going to change the way that person writes poems, more so than just changing line breaks or stanzaic arrangements. Those, to me, are the differences. Something that I've been wind-tunneling, testing really a lot recently, is I used to really feel fairly confident in thinking to myself, most forms don't come with a structural design as well. Sonnets are an exception. Sonnets structure our argument. Argument, argument, turn, counter-argument.

They tell you the form, but then there's a structure that's present as well. That's why a lot of people aren't aware of the kind of rhetorical or ideational structure, and so they go, "Any poem with fourteen lines can be a sonnet." Any poem that does the form will be a sonnet, but it doesn't follow the structure. Several other poem forms have similar kind of structural work, but still recognizing that there's a distinction between putting on the clothes and doing the job.

MALCOLM: There's a lot of writers in the house, of course. This is from Lauren Alleyne. "Is there a distinction to be made between body and voice in these performative encounters? Is the voice wielded only as an extension of the body or is it a different dimension of the engagement?"

DOUGLAS: Oooo. Okay, okay, so: The body and the voice, that is a fantastic question. I'm going to think about it like this. Imagine a duet. You have two people who sing together all the time. Let's not even make it a duet. Let's get out of the world of a binary. Think about the moment in the Emotions' "Best of My Love," when we're getting to that part where we have the lead going, "Oh, oh oh oh oh, oh," and the background singers are going, "Du-uu-uu, du-uu-uu, du-uu-uu, du-uu-uu,-u: Ow!" In that moment, all the background singers hit that "Ow!" and the lead goes, "Ah ah-aah." [SINGS] I'm sorry, I can't hit that note anymore because of all the shouting. But: in that moment, imagine that the body and the voice work together until you need them to separate. In that moment, if you give the listener, the receiver—I'm going to stop saying "listener." I'm sitting here looking at Cynthia Norman [the ASL interpreter]. If you give the audience this moment where you are presenting them with your body—I'll give you an example. There's a poem I do called "Big Thicket, Pastoral." That poem is about James Byrd Jr., who was dragged behind a truck in Jasper, Texas. [DK GETS DOWN ON THE FLOOR, TAKING THE LAPTOP WITH HIM] When I introduce this poem, what I do is I show people how he was dragged.

I tell people that if that door is the back of the truck, his feet are chained behind him, and he's dragged like this. I'm going to try to give you as much angle as I can. His body is being pulled behind a truck with his feet behind him.

Now, I can describe that to you, but something happens at a poetry reading when the poet moves away from the lectern and lies down on the floor.

In that moment, I am using, physically, my body as though to illustrate something that my voice can't do, but I'm drawing attention to my body, with my voice acting in support of that maneuver.

The introduction of that poem is very different if I don't get on the floor. It makes the poem something transformed. Lauren, this is my big concern, and maybe you're thinking something similar, I don't know, but one of the other ideas that is undergirding this lecture, and these questions, and these concerns is that I am a poet who is generally writing about the intersection of violence on Black people, Black women, Black men, Black children, Black trans people, Black young people, Black old people, Black people, and how that is used as a spectacle. How that intersects with entertainment and pleasurable viewing.

Then I go out, and I perform my ass off doing that.

Now, that tension, ain't shit new in Afro-diasporic, US American art, but my body being present up there as a kind of object, as a kind of vessel, kind of butterscotch bonbon, I don't know, fuck—is complicated. [CHUCKLES] It feels funny, yet, voice for Black people—it's hard to decide whether voice is a synecdoche for Black people or a metonym, because for it to be a synecdoche, you'd have to acknowledge there's something else there.

I think, oh that, yes, dear Erica. [DK WAS READING A CHAT MESSAGE] I think for me, this idea of "they work in concert" is really important. Sometimes one takes the solo, but if you look, if you can sense it and a presence of them, if there is a way for you to receive the body and the sound it makes, through whatever mediation is available to you, their mutual presence, I think they are taken in, and the body will be immediately absorbed, taken in as soon as you walk in. As long as you maintain the conventions of the poetry reading, your body can have the same kind of [INAUDIBLE] that the audience gets.

We know that for many people in this Zoom, their very body is a violation of the rules of poetry reading the moment they walk in, even if they stand there right behind the lectern. The question, I think, becomes: If the voice and the body are in concert, is it a group? Is it a duet? How many solos is it? How can we flex that tension? How can we make our bodiness more available, and more importantly, who needs to make their bodiness more available? Some people have had to do without even asking, certainly without wanting to. I don't even know if that answers the question, but it's something that—

MALCOLM: Chad is saying that you answered the question. We're going to take two or three more. Cynthia has been throwing hands for a long time, [LAUGHTER] and Douglas has been talking for a long time. Seeing you getting on the floor and do that movement, giving us that sample, reminded me of when me and Jonah—you talk about Jonah a lot in the lecture—me and Jonah were reading in Ann Arbor, Michigan, and Jonah, as you know, does this poem where he simulates a lynching basically. He turns his face. I know that he was going to do that, but my friend, who's not a poet and isn't familiar with his work, when he did it, she jumped, and then she had to look away because she was like, "This has kind of scared me."

DOUGLAS: [SINGS] "Look awaaaay, look awaaaay, look awaaay."

MALCOLM: Yes. [CHUCKLES] The question is sent to us from someone, no name. They were wondering if you could speak to the role of fear, as in, the audience being scared of you or you being scared of yourself.

DOUGLAS: I don't get to be scared of the audience?

MALCOLM: Sure, yes.

DOUGLAS: [LAUGHS] It's all that, right?

It goes back to the self-care thing. You know those binder clips? This is a Zoom full of writers and people who care for writers, I imagine.

MALCOLM: Like the big ones that you put on scripts sometimes?

DOUGLAS: Yes, yes. I was in Chicago and I was about to do a set of poems. I had a binder clip on my poems and I took it off so I could access them more easily. My hand—I was holding the binder clip, and I was moving the clip because I had to put it someplace. I was like, "Put this on your lip, put it on your lip." Not in like, "The devil made me do it," kind of way, but it was like, "Okay, this makes sense." The whole exchange, going back to Lauren's question, about me speaking. What happens if I harm a spot? Now, if I start taking it up there, and then I go, "Ugh," [DK FEINTS CLIPPING HIS LIP WITH THE BINDER CLIP] that, to me, would feel like a gesture toward breaking the space. Then me like, "No, no. This is a poetry reading, act right." I just put it up there, just in my head was like, "I've never done this before. I hope it doesn't really hurt."

That's not care. On the one hand, that's not protecting myself at all. That's not motivated by fear of the audience. It is motivated, in that moment, by a sense, on the one hand, if I want to talk about aesthetics, it's motivated by a sense of trying to make physical something that would be literary. It's also motivated by a sense of what it means to do gigs, and gigs, and gigs, and be away from my family, away from my family, and away from my family, but need to do the gigs to support my family. The kind of sense of erosion and the kind of sense of, What would it take for me to stop traveling? It turns out: a fucking pandemic.

Fear from the audience? Yes, you get that, but you see, this is the thing I've always thought about in terms of that fear. Most people, in the United States, who absorb US media, so that would include us, that would include Black people. I'm looking at us and thinking Cave Canem, looking at people on the screen. One thing that we are taught is to fear Black people. You can dicker over the details of who are the scariest that we're taught to fear, but generally speaking, we're taught to fear them.

I became aware, at one point, when I was living in the Twin Cities, I used to do poetry readings with my boy, Bao Phi, a brilliant poet. Reps the Asian diaspora, Viet poet.

MALCOLM: I think Bao Phi is here tonight, actually.

DOUGLAS: Oh God, yes. Okay, so Bao is up there? Right.

MALCOLM: I think I saw him out there.

DOUGLAS: Bao does that shit, and we had very similar styles. He was doper than I was, but we had very similar styles. We would sometimes do readings together, and after the readings, both very aggressive and like, "Arrgh!" We do readings, and people walk in like, "Oh, that was so brave." Like that. And people'd come up to Bao and be like, "That was reverse racist."

I began to think about it. If you are expecting to be afraid of Black people and you go to a reading, and there is a Black person yelling at you scarily the whole time, it's like going to a horror movie or riding a roller coaster. You get this little, "Whoooo. Okay, all right, cool." You also get the bonus of, "Hey, I'm not a racist like my uncle. I went there on purpose and let myself be yelled at."

Also, there was something else about it, that it wasn't just thinking outwardly. It was like, I'm not just mad, I'm also terrified, I'm scared, I'm fucking lonely. I'm like, this is cruel, I don't know how to deal with that.

So that became all wedded into it at just an emotional level, and after the emotional level, it became an aesthetic thing. The aesthetic began to amplify the emotion. The fear of going into a space and encountering an audience and not knowing what it means to be in that space, but also knowing that as long as I do what happens in a poetry reading, I feel like everybody's kinda ready for what that's like. Even if my poems are—Even if I yell and spit, or get on the floor sometimes, people are ready for that. Especially if I go, "I'm about to do this poem, get ready." If I walk into the room, and from the outset, the rules of poetry readings, it's like this isn't a poetry reading anymore, I feel like everybody's off-balance. And then I'm the only one who really has a sense of what might be about to happen, because even as I was sprinting toward that wall, I ain't got the same out-the-block speed I used to have. Fifty feet ain't that far. I made these decisions really quickly and decided, no, hit the wall. Nobody else knew it was going to happen.

So fear of myself—because that was a part of the question. It's an important part of the question. I do wonder—switching to Zoom has helped nip that in the bud. I did wonder at what point was I going to possibly actually hurt myself. The audience being afraid of me, that kind of destabilized the situation. [LAUGHS] Not for the reasons you'd expect to be afraid of me.

MALCOLM: Someone asked this question, and I don't know what it means, but maybe you do. If you don't know, we'll just move on. [CHUCKLES] I'm interested because I don't know what to make of it. "Can you say something about minimalism versus maximalism in performance as you constructed this lecture and how minimalism and maximalism inflect race differently?"

DOUGLAS: Oh, yeah, yeah, yeah, I think I understand some of that. If we think of maximalism as a kind of excess, there are many people who argue that a part of the signification of Blackness is a signification of a kind of excess. It's doing a lot. It's that muchness. I didn't want to say anything like this before the Zoom because I didn't want to hex that shit, but I was going to make a joke about that Teddy Riley "Verzuz" thing. [CHUCKLES] I was like, I should have brought my sweat suit and my hat, but I didn't want to jinx it. That sense of "doing a lot."

If you go back to someone like Zora Neale Hurston's "Characteristics of Negro Expression," ehhhhhh—which is an early twenti-eth-century anthropological text on Black culture. Start there. A lot of it spins toward [excess] as a mode of signification, and yet you also have to do this idea of what "cool" is, which might be seeing something more as like a minimalism, like a drawing back, like only giving the bare minimum of what's necessary, as kind of offering and that having to be enough. That tension, I think, between the idea of maximalism/minimalism as being seen as two—for some people—opposing ways of signing Blackness. For some people, there's difficulty trying to, I guess we could say, reconcile those two things, but I always think of this line from "Humble Mumble" by Outkast when Dre says, "I met a critic, I made her shit her drawers. She said she thought hip-hop was only guns and alcohol. I said, 'Oh hell no! But yet it's that, too.'" Like that "Oh hell no! But yet it's that, too." Like that idea of the construction of racial representation. To think about that and then to not think of them strictly as polar opposites but to think about them as available strategies at any given point, like, What does it mean to have a bunch of chains, a madly patterned shirt, baggy jeans, but then just bright white sneakers? That the sneakers are just white.

Now, as a whole, you might look at the picture and be like "Max-imalist," but is that person looking at that arrangement and going like, "Maximal, maximal, minimal," and seeing this constant con-vergence and movement and shifting of signs? And that's something, that kind of work; that sort of asymmetry is something that Zora Neale Hurston talks about in "Characteristics of Negro Expression."

Whenever I start to think about a binary, I think it's useful to be-gin thinking about asymmetry. What do you do with a lean? If you're leaning and you're trying to create a line that your sense of that is going to be all effed up. For me, I think that's one of the ways I think about it. In constructing the lecture, I definitely think that for some people, banter is whittled down to all that you need to say. I've done banter, like the clip I showed, which was this moment of just like—I didn't plan that. It was freely associated, like I said. I just didn't stop myself from saying it.

At the same time, I've also said, "Here's a peppy poem about the Middle Passage: 'Swimchant for Nigger Mer-Folk,'" and just go on. Now, linguistically, in terms of the amount of speech, that might be considered minimalist, but the excess of signifying in the phrase "peppy poem about the Middle Passage," is that maximalist information? Both of those things feel Black to me, the fact that they're happening simultaneously. That's how I'd think about that question, and just the fact that the second you try to pin down people, like that kid from *The Last Dragon* popping and locking out of that shit.

MALCOLM: Great.

DOUGLAS: There's lots of questions, and I'll take a long time to answer the questions. I can try and do a lightning round, because I don't want people to feel like I'm just ignoring questions.

MALCOLM: It's like twenty questions, and some of them are similar.

DOUGLAS: Okay, I'm going to try to be fast, though. I'm going to try to be fast and answer some more questions, because people have stuff to do.

MALCOLM: Okay, in that case, we'll do one to two more.

[LAUGHTER]

DOUGLAS: Your faith in me is astonishing.

MALCOLM: Yeah—Okay . . .

DOUGLAS: [LAUGHTER]

MALCOLM: Before I continue, I've got to remind people that Cave Canem is a nonprofit serving poets worldwide. Even though we're based in Brooklyn, we have over 400 fellows, over thirty faculty, and I think over 900 people have been serviced in our workshops in New York City. You can go to our website; I also dropped the link in the chat to make a donation to Cave Canem to ensure the future of Black poets and future Douglas Kearneys.

Also, as we're doing the final question or two, I'll be dropping into the chat links to buy Douglas's books from Black Garnet. Cynthia Norman's information; as you can see, she's out here doing the work. Also links to Douglas's event with City of Asylum and the website to the Bagley Wright Lecture Series, where you can see other lectures like this; they have an archive on their website. This next question is, "If the poem serves as a kind of intervention and documentation, would you consider the poet to be only a witness? Is the vessel of the poem also there to be a juror and/or judge?"

DOUGLAS: Oh, oh, okay. Read that one more 'gain.

MALCOLM: Okay. Wait, where'd it go? "If the poem serves as a kind of intervention and documentation, would you consider the poet to be only a witness? Is the vessel of the poem also there to be a juror and/or judge?"

DOUGLAS: Okay. So I'm going to just want to specify and untangle something just to make sure, and if this is your question, I'm going to watch the chat just to see if I got it right. When you say, "Is the vessel of the poem also a juror or judge?"—okay. Do you mean, is the poem itself also a juror or judge, or is the poet writing the poem also a juror or a judge? I just want to make sure I got that right. The poem itself or the poet juror or judge, because I can see a really useful intervention—Oh, you're trying to figure it out—okay.

Okay, so like, if the poet—and I'm going to answer this quickly, not because I don't think it's a complex question. If the poet is also a juror or judge of what the poem contains, because the poet is a vessel or a conduit for the poem as a phenomenon for the poetic, as a phenomenon that makes the poem, the poetry reading can be a place where the poet takes the poem, shares it with the people to try to make sense of what they feel the poem does, right?

That becomes that question, I think, of judgment. This gets complicated, I think, once the poet has moved from the manuscript to the published book and does a book tour, because one might then call a distinction between what are the things that drive a poet to decide this [poem's] not ready versus this one is ready to be bound culturally, more permanently as an expression that says, "I judged this one ready." That would be one question about that. This is not saying it can't be that. That would be like, if that's what it does, what do we do with that moment? If that's something that we say, well, a poet for their entire career is still judging whether the poem is to be seen as worthy or not. I think that there are some poets who probably feel that way. I do wonder how many poets do feel that way when they read the poem that has been published. That's a really rich and curious question.

Now, if the poem itself is now also making a judgment, if the poem comes to us and we receive it and the main difference between a person who writes a poem—I'm not going to say poets: a person who writes a poem is a person who is willing to receive that poem and put it down. Then how does that poem's relationship to that writer influence the process of revision, rewriting, and the drive to read the poem aloud or make public in any other way? Let's just say, make public.

Because I think that becomes the question, because then if the poem itself can judge or critique, then the poem has something like —and I'm using "like," and people who know me know that "like" similes make me, like, nervous [CHUCKLES]—then there's something about a consciousness around the poem itself if the poem can judge. What now is the relation between the poem as a somehow conscious entity and the vessel who has been willing to write it down? That, to me, would be the pivot point. The one on the hands of the poet trying to make the judgment call, in some ways, that's more mundane but no less interesting. It's mundane, in that you could talk to poets and be like, "When do you feel like a poem is done?" In some ways, that's the root of that question maybe, or when do you feel like you can stop reading a poem or when have you ever had a poem that you've wanted to pull out or that kind of a thing? There's a question that might be in some ways easier to walk around and ask poets around.

The other question, though, is: is the poem itself a pattern of knowledge-making, decision-making that would operate independently of the specific writer who has it? At what point is the writer reading, caretaking, facilitating, birthing ... but that's a fantastic question.

If you want to argue the consciousness of a poem and take that to its full extension—and that's why I'm always a little bit nervous about metaphors and similes, because people want to use them just a little bit, they want to play—play with them. One of the lectures

I'm working on is "Metaphor Is a Magical Negro Factory," because we oftentimes just want the metaphor to support our life and not go home to their kids. If you want to take it to its full extent, then you'd have to really think about the poem: is it a conscious entity that could judge?

The last thing I'll say about that is, Greil Marcus, the critic, says that the role of the prophet is not necessarily to see the future. The role of the prophet is to make judgments. The poetry reading as an institution is different, I'd say, from the act of experiencing a poem, period, but that's another matter.

Malcolm was right. Malcolm is like, "You ain't gon' be quick. Answer this damn question." If the questions were boring, or really simple. [LAUGHS]

MALCOLM: This is the last question.

[LAUGHTER]

DOUGLAS: Thank you.

MALCOLM: This is from Jubi. I'm going to try to say this correctly. I'm just going to read it and then try to fill in. "What's the cost of engaging the audience and moment in space into the weaving of a poem? Do you divest yourself of reaction or is that part of the poem? I'm thinking back to that moment at AWP 2019 with you and Jonah Mixon-Webster. I left feeling that I had been transformed in some way, but I also left feeling like that was emphatically not the experience of too many of those present. 'This is not a show,' you said, which might be my own projection, but either way, should I give a shit? Should the poet give a shit?"

DOUGLAS: Jubi misquotes me. I said, "This is not a *fucking* show." I said, "This is not a fucking show." That's the only thing I will correct you on, Jubi. That's it. I saw Jonah's performance, as channeling—as Jonah's *intervention* into the conference hotel center of Portland. The cost and the reaction when Jonah *did* that—I'm going to use vernacular, because that'll cover it—when Jonah *did* that, I wanted to stop Jonah, but it was not my right. So, I decided that what I could do was try to protect Jonah, but that might sound presumptuous. Jonah might be on this chat. I was supposed to go after Jonah and do my presentation. And during Jonah's presentation, I was like, "That's not what needs to happen."

First, I wanted to make sure that Jonah was okay. And I was angry, because I thought I might have known a modicum, a tiny—a jot of the cost. I wanted to make sure that the people there understood that it came with a cost and that it wasn't—The fact that Jonah paid the cost does not equal Jonah's treat: "It's on Jonah!" It also does not equal Jonah's sacrifice for you.

I did not presume to know everything about what Jonah did. All I felt I knew was that, (A), it was not a fucking show, it was not designed to be cathartic. I said this, I said, "If anybody feels like they've experienced some catharsis or if they feel like it was a show, get the fuck out now. I'm going to turn around, no shame, but you got to get out, because that's not what this is. It's okay, but you got to go."

Then there was a guy in the audience that I went back and forth with a little bit about this, who was trying to unpack what I meant by "it's not a show," and he was irritated by me saying that and cussing him out, and telling him that he should get out, because maybe he felt that I was just being rude. I felt like, No, I don't give a—. Like, "Do you see?" When I write something, of course, there are moments when I write something where I go, "Oh, when I get to this moment, big things are going—." Like, "This is the moment." I'm composing a poem. I'm putting the words in places and I want that to create things. I want them to create them without me having to be there, though. Part of the reason why I write opera is because I can't sing opera. So, damn it, it's a way that I can write something and I know I don't have to show up and do it.

That's just the facts, y'all.

That doesn't mean that I don't ever want to come into a room and read my work. There are things that I've written where I know exactly who I want to get on the phone with and be like, "Listen, I feel like a kid." Being like, "Can I read this to you? How was your day? Yes, okay, that's interesting. Can I read you this poem?" I feel that, and there are spaces where I want to be, and Q&A's—as y'all probably can guess, I enjoy them. I like being in the space. It's not an "or," it's an "and."

So: There are those moments, and I think about the cost. I've started writing poems like—here, I'll show y'all something. It hasn't even really been out yet. I think it's on this computer.

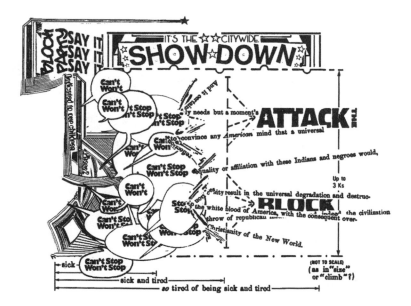

Yes, so this I wrote in June 2020, so I think we all know what that means. That's a poem for a series of poems that are rhetorical armor based upon music forms. It's a shield. The piece is called "Block Party, Say It," and it's a chant shield. It's a shield of chant.

I'm never going to read this aloud. I'm never going to read this poem aloud.

I'm totally happy if I go someplace and somebody says, "Hey, we want to read it aloud," or, "We've come up with a way to read it aloud." That's fine.

I don't have any interest in reading this aloud, and a part of it is: *technically*, I don't want to read it aloud because I think that anything I would do would get in the way of this poem, I think it would harm the poem. There's too many things and this system to the way that my poetics—that I just look at this and, like, "Nope, not interested in reading that aloud." That's one way of getting my body out of it, of changing the cost metric.

I think about it. But here's the thing—and this is the people up in this room, this Zoom. And I don't know if Toi Derricotte is still in here, but Toi Derricotte said something to me, gosh, almost twenty years ago while I was interviewing her for the Loft, which is a literary center in the Twin Cities, in Minneapolis, specifically. She said, "When your fingers tremble above the keyboard, that's the poem." Which says to me that the poem happens when you least want to write it. The poem is the cost.

MALCOLM: Thank you. That's going to conclude our Q&A and tonight's presentation. Thank you, Douglas, for everything. I also wanted to say earlier, that was probably the best Nina Simone impersonation I've ever heard.

[LAUGHTER]

I love that, and thank you, Cynthia, for being with us for so long and doing all the things. Please contact Cynthia for all your needs. Any last things you want to say, Douglas?

DOUGLAS: Just really thank you all for spending this time with us tonight. Cynthia worked eight times harder than I did, so it's with us, and y'all do not know all the work that Malcolm did to get this working so smoothly tonight. Thank you all for being here.

I write because I need to write, but I make it public because of y'all.

I hope for every one of you, you can find that kind of clarity about what this stuff means. I hope that this was helpful in some kind of way to the people in this Zoom, because so many of you are beloved to me. Please, find safety. I'm not going to say "stay safe," because that would be ignoring fucking facts of history. Find safety. For those of you who are unable to find safety or willing to sacrifice your safety, I'm both sorry and grateful. Thank y'all.

APPENDIX B

AN ASIDE ON COLLABORATION

I was invited by *BOMB* to present one of the lectures. I had only done "Red/Read, Read/Red" once, in Portland. I wished to revisit it.

As we solidified the date, Ellen Welcker told me that *BOMB* wished to pair me with another artist so that we could have a conversation about our respective praxes. Maybe a musician? I instantly proposed: Val Jeanty.

> Val Jeanty, also known as Val-Inc, is an Haitian afrofuturist, composer, turntablist, and professor at Berklee College of Music. Jeanty is a pioneer of the electronic music subgenre Afro-Electronica (also called "Vodou-Electro") incorporating Haitian Vodou rhythms with electronic instruments.

Val and I perform together whenever a portal needs opening. But the thing was, I couldn't imagine how we could hit together with the lecture written as it was. You don't ask Val to lay a nice backing track. With Val, you have to PULL UP.

So, I versioned the lecture for its new form as a collaborative lecture.

To address the performance/texture conundrum I discuss in "You Better Hush," I used screen caps of my actual typed lecture pages in Microsoft Word and a scan of a Chartpak letter sheet (Futura Bold).

There you go.

SELECTED BIBLIOGRAPHY

AND WORKS CITED

Alvergue, José Felipe. *scenery: a lyric*. New York: Fordham University Press, 2020.

Brooks, Gwendolyn. *Blacks*. Chicago: Third World Press, 1987.

Brown, Jericho. *The Tradition*. Port Townsend, WA: Copper Canyon Press, 2019.

Burroughs, CM. *The Vital System*. North Adams, MA: Tupelo Press, 2012.

Clifton, Lucille. *Blessing the Boats: New and Selected Poems 1988–2000*. Rochester, NY: BOA Editions, 2000.

Constantine, Brendan. *Birthday Girl with Possum*. Long Beach, CA: Write Bloody Publishing, 2011.

———. *Letters to Guns*. Pasadena, CA: Red Hen Press, 2009.

Dabydeen, David. *Turner: New and Selected Poems*. Leeds: Peepal Tree Press, 2002.

Gaines, Malik. *Black Performance on the Outskirts of the Left: A History of the Impossible*. New York: New York University Press, 2017.

Guyotat, Pierre. *Eden, Eden, Eden*, translated by Graham Fox. London: Creation Books, 1995.

Hans-Taake, Karl. *The Gévaudan Tragedy: The Disastrous Campaign of a Deported 'Beast.'* National Geographic blog.

Harris, Aleshea. *Is God Is*. New York: 3 Hole Press, 2018.

Hayden, Robert. *Collected Poems*. New York: Liveright Publishing Corporation, 1985.

Homer. *The Iliad of Homer*, translated by Richmond Lattimore. Chicago: University of Chicago Press, 2011.

Hunt, Erica. In *The Politics of Poetic Form: Poetry and Public Policy*, edited by Charles Bernstein. New York: Roof Books, 1986.

Ionesco, Eugène. *The Bald Soprano*, translated by Donald M. Allen. New York: Grove Press, 1965.

Jafa, Arthur. "My Black Death." Hudson, NY: Publication Studio, 2015.

Jefferson, Margo. *On Michael Jackson*. New York: Pantheon Books, 2006.

Jennings, Gary. *Black Magic, White Magic*. New York: Dial Press, 1964.

Johnson, Amaud Jamaul. *Red Summer*. North Adams, MA: Tupelo Press, 2006.

Johnson, James Weldon. *God's Trombones: Seven Negro Sermons in Verse*. New York: Penguin, 1990.

Kachuba, John B. *Shapeshifters: A History*. London: Reaktion Books, 2019.

King, Stephen. *Danse Macabre*. New York: Gallery Books, 2010.

Landis, John. "John Landis on the making of *Michael Jackson's Thriller*: 'I was adamant he couldn't look too hideous.'" *The Guardian*, August 31, 2017. www.theguardian.com/film/2017/aug/31/john-landis-on-the-making-of-michael-jacksons-thriller-i-was-adamant-he-couldnt-look-too-hideous.

———. "How we made *An American Werewolf in London*." *The Guardian*, June 12, 2017. www.theguardian.com/film/2017/jun/12/how-we-made-an-american-werewolf-in-london-john-landis.

Lee, Sueyeun Juliette. In *The Cambridge Companion to Twenty-First-Century American Poetry*, edited by Timothy Yu. Cambridge: Cambridge University Press, 2021.

Long Soldier, Layli. *WHEREAS*. Minneapolis: Graywolf Press, 2017.

Marie, Aurielle. *Gumbo Ya Ya*. Pittsburgh: University of Pittsburgh Press, 2021.

Martin, Dawn Lundy. Introduction to *Is God Is*, by Aleshea Harris. New York: 3 Hole Press, 2018.

Montes, Lara Mimosa. *The Somnambulist*. Providence, RI: Horse Less Press, 2016.

Mullen, Harryette. *Recyclopedia*. Minneapolis: Graywolf Press, 2006.

Nelson, Marilyn. *A Wreath for Emmett Till*. Boston: Houghton Mifflin Harcourt, 2005.

Ouch, Cristina. "Stand-Up Comedy Is Not Dying, Your Privilege Is." *Medium*, August 1, 2018. www.medium.com/@cristinaouch/stand-up-comedy-is-not -dying-your-privilege-is-6714fa511e17.

Owen, Wilfred. *Poems*. New York: Viking Press, 1921.

Philip, M. NourbeSe with Setaey Adamu Boateng. *Zong!* Middletown, CT: Wesleyan University Press, 2008.

Phillips, Carl. *Double Shadow*. New York: Farrar, Straus and Giroux, 2011.

Prince, Stephen. "Beholding Blood Sacrifice in *The Passion of the Christ*: How Real Is Movie Violence?" *Film Quarterly* 59, no. 4 (Summer 2006).

Sharif, Solmaz. *Look*. Minneapolis: Graywolf Press, 2016.

Tamayo, Jennif(f)er. *You Da One*. Blacksburg, VA: Noemi Press, 2017.

Trethewey, Natasha. *Thrall*. Boston: Houghton Mifflin Harcourt, 2012.

Yeats, W. B. *The Collected Works of W. B. Yeats*. New York: Macmillan, 1989.

AUDIO AND VIDEO WORKS

Cooder, Ry. "Hush (Somebody's Calling My Name)." *Crossroads*. Warner Bros., 1986.

Grumpy Andrew's Horror House. "Best Werewolf Transformations." YouTube video, 13:37, January 6, 2020. www.youtube.com/watch?v=-UhrAcqBT1Q.

James, Bob. "Nautilus." *One*. CTI Records, 1974.

Jordan, Neil, director. *The Company of Wolves*. Incorporated Television Company and Palace Pictures, 1984.

Kenny, Jack, director. *Christopher Titus: Born with a Defect*. Combustion Films, 2017.

———. *Christopher Titus: Norman Rockwell Is Bleeding*. Deranged Entertainment and KMW Films, 2004.

Landis, John, director. *Michael Jackson's Thriller*. Optimum Productions, 1983.

———. *An American Werewolf in London*. London: PolyGram Pictures, 1981.

Lewis, Robin Coste. Interview by Rachel Zucker. *Commonplace: Conversations with Poets (and Other People)*, November 7, 2018.

Parry, Madeleine and Jon Olb, director. *Hannah Gadsby: Nanette*. Netflix, 2018.

Public Enemy. "Can't Truss It." *Apocalypse 91 . . . The Enemy Strikes Black*. Def Jam, 1991.

RZA, on Ghostface Killa's song "Daytona 500." *Ironman*. Razor Sharp, 1996.

Wu-Tang Clan. *Enter the Wu-Tang (36 Chambers)*. Loud, 1993.

X Clan. *Xodus*. Polydor, 1992.

9th Wonder (with Murs). "Murray's Revenge." *Murray's Revenge*. Record Collection, 2006.

ACKNOWLEDGMENTS

The Bagley Wright Lecture Series on Poetry supports contemporary poets as they explore in depth their own thinking on poetry and poetics and give a series of lectures resulting from these investigations.

This work evolved from lectures given at the following institutions: "I Killed, I Died: Banter, Self-Destruction, and the Poetry Reading," Cave Canem, via Zoom, September 25, 2020; "#WEREWOLFGOALS," Washington University in St. Louis, via Zoom, October 8, 2020; "Red/Read, Read/Red: Putting Violence Down in Poetry," Portland Literary Arts, OR, via Zoom, March 24, 2021; "You Better Hush: Blacktracking A Visual Poetics," Seattle Arts & Lectures, via Zoom, March 31, 2021; "I Killed, I Died: Banter, Self-Destruction, and the Poetry Reading," Yale University, via Zoom, April 15, 2021; "#WEREWOLF-GOALS," New York University, via Zoom, April 22, 2021; "I Killed, I Died: Banter, Self-Destruction, and the Poetry Reading," the Poetry Project, NY, via Zoom, May 20, 2021; "Red/Read, Read/Red: Version" (with Val Jeanty), *BOMB* & the Ace Hotel, Brooklyn, NY, November 9, 2021.

Thank you to Malcolm H. Tariq, Natalie Desrosiers, and Della Green at Cave Canem; Mary Jo Bang, David Schuman, and Shannon Rabong at Washington University in St. Louis; Susan Moore and Jessica Meza-Torres at Portland Literary Arts; Rebecca Hoogs and Alison Stagner at Seattle Arts & Lectures; Karin Roffman and Gabrielle Colangelo at Yale University; Joanna Yas and Madeleine Mori at New York University; Kyle Dacayun at the Poetry Project; Libby Flores, Bo Suh, Isis Pinheiro, Nichole Almanzar at *BOMB* and Marie van Eersel at the Ace Hotel Brooklyn; and all of their respective teams, for welcoming the Bagley Wright Lecture Series into their programming and for collaborating on these events. The Series would be impossible without such partnerships. Thank you to Cynthia Norman and Billy A. Sanders for providing ASL interpretation throughout.

Douglas Kearney, "The Miscarriage: A List of Ten Euphemisms for Use in Stage Banter" from *Patter*. Copyright © 2014 by Douglas Kearney. Reprinted with the permission of The Permissions Company, LLC on behalf of Red Hen Press, www.redhen.org. "The Cave Canem Q&A" transcript printed with permission of the author and Malcolm H. Tariq.

NOTE FROM THE AUTHOR

I thank Charlie Wright of the Bagley Wright Lecture Series for his incredibly generous and life-changing support. Infinite gratitude to Ellen Welcker, whose patience and brilliant shepherding never ceased throughout this four-year process. Thanks as well to the emcees, tech, and staff of the venues that hosted these lectures.

Thank you to Cynthia Norman (empress!) and Billy Sanders for throwing hands.

Thank you CM Burroughs, LaTasha N. Nevada Diggs, Amaud Jamaul Johnson, Evie Shockley, and Yona Harvey for voting on the list of titles that led to this lecture series.

Thank you to my family for supporting my writing even when it takes me away from you. Nicole, love, you are always my best first editor. E and K, y'all inspire me. Thank you, Ma, for insisting I rest.

To my late parents, rest in joy with each other. I would have loved to share these with you and your parents on this side of things.

Dallas and ChaVon: y'all always lift me up!

To my aunts and uncles, cousins and nephews, thank you for the conversations that give me language and impetus.

I thank my friends for riding with me. And to the writers and other artmakers I name in (and beyond) this book, thank you for challenging, changing, and unsettling me. I hope I do your work justice.

I thank my students, whose thoughtful inquiries made this book a thing. Thanks to my colleagues and teachers (past and present) for sharing intellectual models from which I still learn. And thank you to the staff who everywhere make all things possible.

Thank you to the librarians, whose daily contributions to our lives cannot be praised enough.

To the teams at Wave (Blyss, Catherine, Heidi, Isabel, Joshua, and Matthew), Crisis, and Blue Flower Arts, thank you for your tireless work on my work.

Thank YOU, reader.

And, like in all the moments when I make a connection between two ping-ponging thoughts, I thank God.